THE
BORDER TERRIER

by David VanGordon Kline
and Patricia Bennett Hoffman

DORAL
PUBLISHING

Wilsonville, Oregon
1993

Copyright © 1993 by David VanGordon Kline and Patricia Bennett Hoffman.

Published by Doral Publishing, PO Box 596, Wilsonville OR 97070.
Printed in the United States of America.

Copyedited by Luana Luther.
Cover Design by Palatine Design Group.
Front Cover: Ch. Falcliff Target by D.V. Kline.
Back Cover: Border Terrier Puppy, V. & J. Sabo, 1991.
Drawings by Mary Jung

Library of Congress Card Number: 91-73751
ISBN: 0944875-20-3

Kline, David VanGordon.
  The border terrier / by David VanGordon
Kline and Patricia Bennett Hoffman, —
Wilsonville, OR : Doral Pub., c1993.

  p,262 : ill. ; cm. — (The purebreds)

Includes bibliographical references and
index.
ISBN: 0-944875-20-3

  1. Border terriers. I. Hoffman,
Patricia Bennett. II. Title. III. Series

SF429.B65K   636.7'55 dc20
    91-73751

CONTENTS

Part III — All About the Border Terrier

Part IV — Reference Material

ACKNOWLEDGEMENTS

We thank all the people who have so generously contributed information, photos and encouragement. We are particularly grateful to the friends who have written special sections: Anna-Karin Bergh, Carolyn Dostal, Christopher Habig, Lena Harjapää, Barbara Kemp, Susan Milne, Robert and Ruth Ann Naun, Margaret Pough, Laurale Stern, Rosemary and George Williamson and Connie S. Brunkow.

FOREWORD

Unbeknownst to either of us, Dave and I began in Border Terriers at the same time 25 years ago. At the time, he was living in Iran and returned by way of Britain where he acquired Ch. Rhosmerholme Belinda from Mrs. Edna Garnett and Ch. Falcliff Target from Mr. Ellis Mawson. He quickly finished both in the United States; they are behind most of the top-winning American-breds today, including Dave's present-day Borders. I met Dave at a BTCA Specialty in Greenwich, Connecticut, and we have been great friends since.

Dave grew up with hounds, horses and livestock on his grandfather's farm, and it is from this early association that he developed his love for all animals, and specifically dogs. He began in dogs while in junior high school with Dalmatians and finished some nice ones in that breed. But it was the Border Terrier that became his first love and to which he has devoted his interest through the years. Dave has always been a student of dogs and throughout his life has continued to study structure and anatomy. And, in his early years, he learned from many people who were the greats in dogs and in Border Terriers, most of whom are now deceased. Because he started in dogs while young, Dave has been a sort of link with the past for many.

Dave is an AKC-licensed judge of Border Terriers and has officiated at two BTCA national specialties, Montgomery County, in Britain and at countless other shows throughout the United States. His real interest, however, remains breeding and getting a good one out at the shows, and whenever Dave does show, his Todfield Borders hold their own in the keenest competition.

Patricia Bennett Hoffman, co-author of The Border Terrier in America, has been actively involved in purebred dogs — primarily Mastiffs — for 30 years. She co-authored the definitive book on the breed, The History and Management of the Mastiff, and for many years was a book reviewer for The American Kennel Club Gazette. Patricia has been a long-time aficionado and owner of Border Terriers, importing, breeding and exhibiting a number of the breed.

We in Border Terriers in the United States have long wanted an American book on the breed, and were enthusiastic when we heard that Dave and Patricia were writing one. The book is eagerly awaited by the fancy for the authors' depth of knowledge, love of the breed and their practical approach to breeding, rearing and care.

Nancy J. Hughes
Trails End
West Chicago, Illinois

PART I

Introduction
to the Border Terrier

- *The Background of the Border Terrier*

- *The Border Terrier in the US to 1970*

- *The Border Terrier in the US from 1970 to 1980*

- *The Border Terrier in the US after 1980*

"Earth Stopper," from the Rev. W. B. Daniels' **Rural Sports, 1807.**

CHAPTER 1

The Background
of the Border Terrier

As is true with the majority of Terrier breeds, the origin and history of the Border Terrier are somewhat obscure. A mixture of fact, fiction and legend lies behind the breed as we know it today. Unlike many other breeds, the Border has no highly colored background — it wasn't reported to have crossed the Alps with Hannibal, nor was it depicted on Assyrian bas-reliefs or drawn on the walls of a pharaoh's tomb. The only bit of picturesque lore is the occasional reference to its being owned by gypsies and tinkers in the 1800s.

Many believe that the Border Terrier is descended from a blend of old strains of working Terrier, closely related to the Dandie Dinmont, the Lakeland, and the Bedlington, that originated in the general area of northern England and southern Scotland. For an interesting discussion of the various English Terriers of the past, see David Hancock's book, *Old Working Dogs*. (At the end of this book is a list of suggested additional reading.) He refers to the Border Terrier: "...some of the 'valley' breeds are perpetuated today in the Border Terrier, gamest of earth dogs, brave but never foolishly so." Note the Terrier at the foot of the horseman in the illustration, *The Earth Stopper*. Shown is a small dog strongly resembling the present-day Border. The print is from *Rural Sports*, written by the Rev. W. B. Daniel in 1809.

D.J. Thomson Gray, who wrote under the pen name *Whinstone*, believed the Border to be *the* basic rough-coated Terrier. In his book, *The Dogs of Scotland*, published in 1891, he commented:

> The Border is by no means a rare animal, although confined to a limited area, and to one part of the country, and as regards antiquity may claim to be the original terrier of the hills, from which the

Dandie and Bedlington sprung. Unlike the Dandie and Bedlington, which are a compound of two or more breeds, the Border terrier still retains all its pristine purity. Bred for work and not for show, fancy points are not valued in proportion to working qualities, still the breed has many distinctive features which are carefully preserved...Their intelligent eyes, hard coat, and general activity stamp them as an intelligent breed which has not yet been contaminated and 'improved' by the fancier.

Gray then went on to quote Thomas Robson, whose Northumberland family had long been associated with the breed: "These terriers have been on the Border for generations, and I fancy have as much *original* Dandie blood as the show Dandie of today...Crossed they may have been sometimes, when a good dog of any sort turned up, but they are still true to type."

Additional comments were provided by Edward E. Loch of Bristol. He described the Border as a "hard-haired, short-coated terrier of about 11 or 12 inches at the shoulder, weighing about 17 lbs." Concluding a rather muddled description, he wrote: "Of the pedigree of this dog nothing is known, and in appearance is more like a hard-haired Dandie with semi-erect ears and no top-knot — in fact, looks like a cross between a Dandie and Scottish terrier." Indeed!

Ending his four pages on the Border, Gray wrote: "What little information we have been able to give, we hope, may be the means of drawing attention to the breed and thus prevent its extinction."

Further information appeared in an article printed in the 1952 *Year Book* of the Southern Border Terrier Club (England). James Garrow wrote "Looking Back," in which he said: "It is close on sixty years since I was introduced to the Border Terrier." Reminiscences of some early shows followed this comment:

The breeders were afraid that recognition of the breed by the Kennel Club would ruin it as a working terrier. It, however, did not, and the Border is as game today as it was then. I can say the show bench has not altered the breed in any way and I also maintain that many of the winners of

J. T. Dodds' Flint and Fury, from W. D. Drury, **British Dogs,** *circa 1902.*

fifty years ago could win on the show benches today. There were certainly not so many of the real good ones in those days, but the type has not changed in any way.

The writer then went on to quote a letter from James Dodd, joint-master and secretary of the Haydon Hunt in Border country until 1921:

I can trace the Border Terrier back since the year 1817, bred for work on both sides of the Border. The breeders were not particular as to shape, colour, or form as long as they went to ground and could tackle and bolt a fox. If they could do that they were kept for hunting. There has always been a great controversy as to the origin of the breed, and from information I have gleaned there is not the least doubt but that it has been descended from both the old-fashioned type of Bedlington Terrier and the old crossed type of Dandie Dinmont Terrier. Such ancestry is till very noticeable in the present-day Border. The old type of Bedlington, a nice-sized dog of eleven and one-half lbs. was a handy terrier; just as was the old type Dandie of the same weight. I have some prints of both, taken over one hundred years ago. When all the pros and cons are weighed up there is no doubt but that our Border Terrier is a direct cross between these two varieties. I remember the working Bedlington and the working Dandies having flesh-coloured noses. They were mustard or liver coloured, and these characteristics still crop up amongst some of the Borders. I have had Border Terriers over sixty years, and my grandfather kept them before me.

J. J. Pawson wrote an article, "The Border Terrier," for one of the Year Books of the Southern Border Terrier Club. It was reprinted, without a date, in the 1967 *Border Tales*, a collection of articles from 1947 to 1965. Briefly discussing the history of the breed, he stated:

> The Border Terrier has been the most popular terrier in his native country, Northumberland, for a great number of years. The name was connected with the Border Foxhounds...The Border Foxhounds were under the Mastership from 1870 of Jacob Robson and the Robsons and Dodds after him. They would not have any terriers but the Border to run and work with the foxhounds. In 1920, the Kennel Club first recognized the breed with the result that they became more and more popular in the south of England."

Pointing out that many members of the Southern Club knew little about the breed's history, he went on to say: "It originated about 1817 as a cross between the 'Pepper and Mustard' strain (later known as the Dandie Dinmont) and the strain which was later (in 1825) named the Bedlington." Mr. Pawson, one of the founders of the Southern Club, died in 1965.

A final note on the cloudy origin of the Border is from Robert Leighton's four-volume work, *Cassell's New Book of the Dog* (1927). In the chapter, "The Old Working Terrier," Leighton wrote that the Elterwater Terrier was "not easily distinguishable from the better-known Border Terriers, of which there are still many strains." However, Borders were not listed among his "rough-coated" terriers.

Take your choice of the theories above. Even the name *Border* is of questionable origin. One school of thought attributes it to the fact that the breed hails from the border country of Northumberland and Roxboroughshire. Another belief is that the name comes from the Border Foxhounds, the pack with which Border Terriers were used and which had much to do with their development.

At any rate, the Border, called Coquetdale or Elterwater Terrier until about 1880, was well known as a game little dog. The first instance of his being shown was at a working Terrier show in 1870, in a so-called Variety Class. After this, there were no records of the dogs being shown for several years.

In 1913, a Border was registered with the English Kennel Club. This was The Moss Trooper, listed under *Any Breed or Variety of British, Colonial or Foreign Dog — Not Classified*. Until 1920, only 41 registrations of the breed were made under this classification.

Then a Border Terrier Club, with more than 120 members, was founded and the official Standard drawn up, much as it is today. That year, 1920, the English Kennel Club granted Border Terriers official recognition, to the sorrow of many breeders who felt that the essential working qualities of the dogs were far more important than conformation.

About the same time, the Northumberland Border Terrier Club established its own Standard and kept its own studbook for some years. Their 1921 club show drew an entry of 103 Borders, an astonishing number at any time. This northern club faded out about 1928, and its records were lost, as were those of the English club before 1930, which leads to a certain vagueness as to early proceedings.

For detailed information on the breed in the United Kingdom, the best reference is Anne Roslin-Williams' book, *The Border Terrier*. Her exhaustive chapter, "The Influence of Bloodlines and Kennels," is required reading for those who want to delve into the history of the breed.

Continuing with the history and background of the Border Terrier, let's look at a comparison of the English and American Standards. A more detailed analysis and discussion of our American Standard will be found later in this book.

The American Standard is far longer and goes into greater detail than does the English version. Where we have an extended description and rather lengthy General Appearance, the English Standard states simply:

> *Characteristics — The Border Terrier is essentially a working Terrier. It should be able to follow a horse and must combine activity with gameness.*

Our section on *Head* includes not only the head itself, but also the ears, eyes, muzzle, teeth and nose in minute detail. The British give each of these, except the nose, a separate brief heading, as follows:

Eng. Ch. Dandy of Tynedale, owned by J. Dodd. From C. Sanderson, **Pedigree Dogs,** *1927.*

Head and Skull — Head like that of an otter, moderately broad in skull with a short strong muzzle; a black nose is preferable but a liver or flesh-coloured one is not a serious fault.

Eyes — Dark, with keen expression.

Mouth — Teeth should have a scissor-like grip, with the top teeth slightly in front of the lower, but level mouth is quite acceptable. An undershot or overshot mouth is a major fault and highly undesirable.

The *Neck* is described in just three words: *of moderate length.*

The section on Body is shorter than ours, which states: *a man's hands*, a small but important addition:

Body — Deep and narrow and fairly long; ribs carried well back, but not oversprung, as a Terrier should be capable of being spanned by both hands behind the shoulder.

Our next section is the *Tail*, almost identical with our description but which the English place after *Hindquarters* described as *Racy. Loin strong*, followed by *Feet — Small with thick pads.*

Tail — Moderately short and fairly thick at the base then tapering, set high and carried gaily but not curled over the back.

The American Standard goes into some detail on coat and hide, whereas the English Standard simply states:

Coat — Harsh and thick with close undercoat. The skin must be thick.

The *Color* description allows the same basic colors, but the British do not include the allowance for white that we permit.

And, in conclusion, after the final paragraph on weight of the dogs:

NOTE: Male animals should have two apparently normal testicles fully descended into the scrotum.

Cryptorchidism is an automatic disqualification in all breeds here in the United States..

Of interest are a few sections from the *Standard of Points* drawn up by the Northumberland Club some 70 years ago.

Thirteen topics were given, beginning with the statement: *N.B. The points are placed in order of their importance.*

The Border Terrier should be a real sporting Terrier, and not too big. Weights were specified as a maximum of 14 pounds for dogs, 13 pounds for bitches. The final point, and presumably the least important was: *Mouth, level: undershot or pig-jawed no use.*

To complete these comparisons, a note on the Canadian Standard, which is similar to the one on file with the American Kennel Club. The Border Terrier was first registered in Canada in 1929-1930, but no date is given for its actual recognition there.

CHAPTER 2

The Border Terrier in the United States Before 1970

The history of the Border Terrier in the United States is relatively short. Prior to the breed's recognition by the American Kennel Club in 1930, only 18 Terriers were brought to this country. Of these, only three were ever registered. These were:

Harry S. Cram's *Barney Boy* (Eng. Ch. Dandy of Tyndale x Queen o' the Hunt).
G. C. Thayer's *Nessy* (Arnton Bill x Nessel)
G. C. Thayer's *Blacklyne Lady* (Eng. Ch. Ben of Tweeden x Blacklyne Wasp).

The first registration of a Border Terrier in this country was that of *Netherbyers Ricky* (AKC 719372) owned by Don E. Hewat, bred by Miss E. Hardy of Scotland (Redheugh Rick x Rogie) in 1930. A total of six Borders were registered that first year.

Mr. Cram's *Barney Boy*, who ran with the hounds in South Carolina, was the second entry, and it is interesting to note that his owner was still a member of the Border Terrier Club in 1987.

Barney was followed by four other listings, all owned by Mr. Thayer: *Nessy, Blacklyne Lady, Southam Boy*, who had the same sire and dam as Nessy, and *Southam Girl* (Arnton Billy x Tinkle). One import who was never registered was *Eng. Ch. Rustic Rattler* (Crosedale Jock x Crosedale Judy) — one wonders what he might have contributed to the breed here.

There were no listings with the AKC in 1931, but 1932 brought several, including Cram's *Daisy Belle* (Dryburn Demon x Belle o' the Hunt, bred by Dodd and Carruthers).

L-R: Merritt N. Pope and Mrs. Pope, Scotties and Borders (Philabeg); William MacBain and daughter Kathleen Carpe, Scotties and Borders (Diehard).

And one of the charter members of the breed club, General E.E. Hume, registered *Weddie* (Trooper x Fairloans Fly), and it was the only Border to be shown at the 1934 National Capital Show in Washington, D.C.

G. Gordon Massey owned several of the breed, and he registered the first two American- bred litters in 1931. One was by *Mullach* (Arnton Billy x Anthorn Lady) out of *Always There* (Hunting Boy x June of Twinstead). The other litter, also sired by Mullach, was out of *Dryffe Judy* (Whitrope Don x Eng. Ch. Station Smasher).

In 1937, William MacBain brought over *Pyxie O'Bladnoch*, with *of Diehard* added later (Dandy Warrior x Bladnoch Beatrice, bred by Dr. W. Lillico), who was in whelp to *Eng. Ch. Foxlair*. Then Pyxie was bred to Massey's *Red Twister* (Twempie Tony x Eng. Ch. Todhunter, bred by J. Rendon). From this litter came *Diehard Betta,* whose descendants appear in later Philabeg and Dalquest pedigrees. Otherwise this line died out.

Pyxie became the first champion in the breed in 1941.

Mr. MacBain also imported *Emigrant of Diehard* (Eng. Ch.Dipley Dibs x Wind o' Lammermuir). Emerson Latting acquired *Diehard Dandy* (Diehard Sandy x Diehard Betta) who became the second Border Terrier champion in 1942, and the first American-bred to win the title.

In spite of World War II, two dogs came from England in 1942. These were *Heather Sandy* (Fearsome Fellow x Tishie) and *Bladnoch Blossom* (Red Sunset x Bladnoch Maeve) who mated on the sea voyage to this country and produced four puppies. Mr. Latting owned Blossom and later acquired Heather Sandy from Mr. MacBain.

A few years later, in 1948, the first American-bred bitch champion was *Philabeg Red Miss*, owned and bred by Dr.

Dr. Merritt Pope's Diehard puppies. L-R: Jill, Lovely Lady, Pyxie, Red Miss, Fury. 1941.

Ch. Heather Sandy of Diehard, 1949. Photo by Evelyn M. Shafer.

Ch. Dalquest Dangerous Dan, 1951. Photo by Evelyn M. Shafer.

Ch. Raisgill Romper of Philabeg, 1952.

Philabeg Duchess, CD. First Border Terrier to win Companion Dog degree, 1953.

Merritt N. Pope (Diehard Laddie x Diehard Jill). In 1947, Dalquest Kennels acquired their first Border Terrier from Dr. Pope. This was **Philabeg Red Bet**, and was the beginning of Marjorie L. Van der Veer's and Margery Harvey's long association with Border Terriers. With these two kennels, Philabeg and Dalquest, as well as Mr. MacBain's Diehard, the breed was becoming well established.

This brings our account up to the founding of the Border Terrier Club of America. After some discussion in 1946, a preliminary organization was formed at the 1947 Westminster Kennel Club Show in New York, with Dr. Pope as chairman.

In 1948, a Standard was drawn up and submitted to the American Kennel Club. The following year the club was formally organized, with 10 members. The president was Dr. Pope; vice-president, Capt. John C. Nicholson; treasurer, Mrs. Nicholson; and the secretary was Miss Van der Veer, a position she was to hold for 34 years. A constitution and by-laws were drawn up, and in 1950, the Standard of the Breed was accepted by the American Kennel Club.

From that time on, Border affairs moved rapidly. In 1952, Dr. Pope's import, **Ch. Raisgill Romper of Philabeg** achieved a placing in the Terrier Group — a notable event. The dog was bred by H. G. Orme, by **Eng. Ch. Boxer Boy** out of **Raisgill Ruth**.

Another important first was the winning of the Companion Dog title by Mrs. Anthony Cerasale's **Philabeg Duchess** in 1953. Duchess was sired by **Romper** out of **Princess of Philabeg**, bred by Dr. Pope.

In 1986, Patricia Cerasale Loll wrote an account of Duchess:

> Our first Border was Philabeg Duchess, a six month old bitch puppy that we bought from Dr. Merritt N. Pope of Philabeg Kennels in Virginia. Her sire was Raisgill Romper of Philabeg, an imported dog, and her dam was Dr. Pope's Princess of Philabeg. She was a rather quiet, reserved older puppy, and probably a little large for a bitch; Dr. Pope sold her to us basically as a pet.

Ch. Portholme Max Factor, 1954.

But Duchess had a few problems fitting into a family; she wasn't sure what to do about two small children who were constantly wanting to pet her and hold her, and she was shy with visitors, and would nip at their heels as they left the house.....And, against the better judgement of the breeder, mom and Duchess started Obedience training.

The results were electric. Duchess' entire attitude changed; and when at her first Obedience Trial at the National Capital KC show, on March 15, 1953, she scored a 190 and proceeded to go BOB against three other Border bitches.... Dr. Pope's attitude changed, too — he became a believer in Obedience training for terriers.

Ch. Dour Dare, 1957. Photo by Evelyn M. Shafer.

Ch. Dalquest Dauntless, 1960. Photo by Frasie.

Ch. Cinjola Buddy Boy Dauntless, 1961. Photo by Frasie.

The breed club became more and more active and in 1954, the first *Breed Booklet* was published with 500 copies. Its editors were Miss Harvey, Miss Van der Veer, and Dr. Pope. Priced at one dollar, it had 52 pages. The Standard was printed with comments by Dr. Pope. There were four pages of photographs,"Illustrations of Good Border Terrier Points," chosen by Miss Hester Garnet-Orme with accompanying commentary. Miss Garnet-Orme also wrote "Founding the Kennel."

Other material included an article by an English judge, James Garrow, with a little history of the breed in England; "The All Purpose Terrier" by Barbara M. L. Eccles of England, which emphasized the working aspects of the breed; and a delightful account by Miss Van der Veer, "The Border Terrier as A Companion," in which she wrote: "Wherever he may be, the Border fits in neatly without fuss and adapts himself to his environment.... the Border has come down through the years unspoiled by his admirers, in either appearance or spirit.....He is hardy, clean and with proper care, food and exercise is very long lived."

There was a complete list of champions up to that date, 12 in all, plus the one Obedience Title holder. Six pages of ads from various members, other articles, membership list and so forth complete the very large amount of information packed into this first effort by the club.

Other events of 1954 included the first appearance of the Border Terrier breed column in the American Kennel Club *Gazette* as a Non-Member Club and the publication of the first club newsletter. Both were written by Miss Van der Veer (who continued as *Gazette* writer until 1989). She continued to edit the *Newsletter* until 1974, when it became *The Borderline* in printed format under the editorship of David V. Kline, who held the position until 1977, when the present editor, Patricia Quinn, took over. The cover of the June 1954 *Gazette* featured two Borders, **Dalquest Red Robin** and **Dalquest Red Duchess**. Four champions were made up that year.

Borders continued to win titles, two champions in 1955 and three the following year. In 1956, the first of the breed to win both English and American championships was **Lucky Purchase** (Eng. Ch. Future Folly x Fully Fashioned), bred by Mr. and Mrs. A. Forster and owned by Kate Webb.

In 1957, the club held its first Plan "A" Sanctioned Match, in preparation for the first Specialty Show. The match was held April 27 at Marion duPont Scott's estate Montpelier. Heywood Hartley was the judge, and his choice for winner from the 20 entries was **Dalquest Derry Down**, a bitch owned by Carroll K. Bassett. Bred by Margery Harvey, her sire was **Ch. Portholme Max Factor** and her dam was **Ch. Dour Dare**. Interest in the breed was growing, and 53 were registered that year.

The 1958 "A" Match took place May 19 at the Piping Rock Club on Long Island. As the show date was on a Monday, the entry dropped to 13. Frank Brumby judged, and awarded Best in Match to Warner Jones's **Shelburne Jonesie** (Ch. Portholm Max Factor x Ch. Golden Fancy, bred by Kate J. Webb).

The year 1958 witnessed a number of important events in the breed. The *Second Breed Booklet* was published. It was free to the club's 52 members, $1.50 to others. Its 80 pages had the usual lists of officers and members; the Standard; and various articles. Two were by the club president, Dr. Pope: "How the Border Differs from Other Terriers" and "Justification of the Breed Standard." There were several articles by both English and American owners on hunting, and one by Miss Van der Veer on handling. All champions to the date of publication were listed, and photographs and pedigrees of numbers 13 through 30 were given. Three champions finished in 1956, and six in 1958. There were no CD awards since the first won by Philabeg Duchess in 1953.

The article and photos of correct Border types were reprinted from the *First Breed Booklet*, and there were a number of pictures of English champions and holders of Working Certificates. On the lighter side, an article on a remarkable Border named *Paddy Reilly*, was reprinted from the AKC *Gazette*, telling of his exploits, which included reportedly having saved a number of lives as well as collecting a large amount of money for the Greenwich Village (NY) Humane Society.

Also in 1958, Marion duPont Scott finished her first champion, imported *Carahall Cindylou* (Eng. Ch. Carahall Cornet x Carahall Charm), and her first home-bred champion, *Nancy* (Ch. Portholme Manly Boy x Ch. Carahall Cindylou).

The Border Terrier Club of America's first Specialty Show was held May 16, 1959, in conjunction with the Ladies Kennel Association, Garden City, Long Island. It remained at that show for the following five years. Haywood R. Hartley judged the 31 entries. Dalquest Kennels had a day of triumph, as their *Ch. Portholme Mhor of Dalquest* (Portholme Mustard x Eng. Ch. Portholme Mirth) was Best of Breed. Their *Ch. Dalquest Smokey Tigress* (Dalquest Merry Mike x Dalquest Dusty Dinah) won Best of Opposite Sex.

In addition to the first kennels — Philabeg, Diehard, Dalquest — several other kennels played an important part in advancing the breed in the 1950s. The Borders of Montpelier came on the scene in the middle of the decade. Although Marion duPont Scott did not have a kennel name, Carroll Bassett used Toftwold. Their dogs were of great influence on the breed. Mrs. Scott's first Border was *Wallace*, born in 1953 (Ch. Raisgill Romper x Hark), and he was always her favorite. For many years, Mrs. Scott held a lavish birthday party for him, entertaining dogs and owners at her estate. The first BTCA Match was held there, on a date as close to Wallace's birthday as possible.

In 1955, Mrs. Scott bought *Dalquest Derry Down* (Ch. Portholme Max Factor x Ch. Dour Dare) and gave the bitch to Mr. Bassett, who made her a champion in 1957. Later imports were, among others, *Ch. Carahall Cindylou*, who arrived in whelp to En. Ch. Portholme Manly Boy; *Leatty Lucky Girl*; *Solway Athol Brose*; *Solway Hot Toddy*; the 1961 champion, *Leatty Lucky Gift* (Ch. Leatty Jean's Laddie x Leatty Miss Merry). Mr. Bassett brought in *Leatty Jean's Laddie* (Eng. Ch. Leatty Druridge Dazzler x Queen's Beauty), a 1957 champion. Other important sires from Montpelier were *Ch. Dalquest Mhor's Golden Gloves* (Ch. Portholme Mhor of Dalquest x Ch. Porthome Bellarina of Dalquest) and the 1962 import, *Ch. Koffee Lad* (Alton Lad x Linwell).

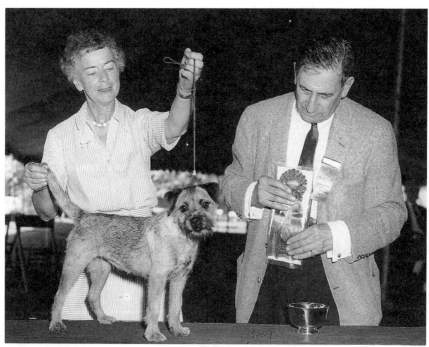

Ch. Dalquest Image of Tige, 1962. Photo by Evelyn M. Shafer.

Ch. Portholme Macsleap of Dalquest, 1965.

Mex. and Am. Ch. Bandersnatch Brillig, CD. Painting by Dale Gourlie.

Mrs. Scott was a generous supporter of the club from the date she joined in 1956 until her death in 1984. She was patron of several of the club publications and donated a large number of trophies.

Another early fancier who is still active is Mrs. Kate J. Webb, later Kate Seemann, whose kennel name *Shelburne* appears in many pedigrees. Her first home-bred champion was **Shelburne Slipper** (Bottles x Golden Fancy) in 1956. That same year her imported **Lucky Purchase** lived up to his name by becoming the first Border Terrier to hold both English and American titles as mentioned earlier. Mrs. Seemann has held various positions with the club, including the office of president from 1960 to 1965, and has donated many trophies.

The Montpelier Borders had great success at the 1960 Club Specialty Show. Mrs. Scott's **Ch. Bruce** (Wallace x Ch. Carahall Cindylou) was Best of Breed, and his dam was Best of Opposite Sex. Percy Roberts was the judge of the 27 entries. That year there was a second Companion Dog title awarded. This was to *Philabeg Impetuous* (Raisgill Rash x Dour Diane), bred by Dr. Pope and owned by Frieda Kenyon . Club membership was 48.

The first two Borders owned by *Cinjola* Kennels became champions in 1960. These were **Dalquest Dauntless** (Ch. Portholme Mhor of Dalquest x Ch. Portholme Meroe) and **Dalquest Dare's Dancer** (Portholme Max Factor x Ch. Dour Dare). These two were the parents of **Cinjola Little Donk**, the kennel's first home-bred champion in 1961. Cinjola, located in Indiana, was owned by John and Ethel Barker and Mrs. Barker's sister, Pearlene Smith. Mrs. Barker, a medical technician, named many of her Borders after dye solutions used in staining slides — thus **Cinjola's Aurentia Red**, a 1964 champion, also from the Dalquest foundation stock. This was also the first American-bred bitch to win a Group placing.

In 1961, Kate Webb's **Eng. and Am. Champion Dandyhow Bitter Shandy** (Fighting Fettle x Walla Crag Wendy) became the first bitch of the breed to win a Group placing. She also won the club show that year under Terence P. Bresnahan. The Best of Opposite Sex was **Dalquest's Ch. Portholme Mhor of Dalquest** (Portholme Mustard x Eng. Ch. Portholme Mirth), from 27 entries. Another 1961 event was the first American-bred dog to win a Group placement. This was **Dalquest Auburn Lad**, owned by John A. Caple. Despite this win, the dog never went on to become a champion.

The third *Breed Booklet* was published in 1962; it had 89 pages and sold for two dollars. It featured Border Terrier champions 31 through 67, with photographs and pedigrees. Editor Van der Veer contributed a detailed history of the club. Included were the usual list of officers, trophies, and other club topics, plus a number of articles ranging from how to choose a puppy to health problems. Mrs. Henry B. Lent, Jr., contributed "The Borders of Lent At Work," describing hunting woodchucks with her dogs, and giving hints on training for hunting. Later, in 1971, Mrs. Lent was founder of the American Working Terrier Association.

The 1962 Specialty was won by Mrs. Scott's **Ch. Koffee Lad** (Alton Lad x Linwell, an import bred by T. M. Gaddes). There were 23 entries, and Judge Alva Rosenberg gave Mrs. Webb's **Ch. Dandyhow Bitter Shandy** Best of Opposite Sex. Twelve Borders finished their championships that year.

Ch. Bull Run, 1968.

The 1963 Specialty had a very small entry, only 13. Mrs. Webb's *Eng. and Am. Ch. Jonty Lad* (Tourist x Eng. Ch. Primrose) won, and Judge Chris Shuttleworth awarded Best of Opposite Sex to *Ch. Mied Auburn Lass's Heather* (Ch. Portholme Mhor of Dalquest x Ch. Dalquest Auburn Lass) bred and owned by Edmund and Mildred Shaw. There were four champions that year, plus one Companion Dog title.

In 1964, the Specialty moved to the Greenwich (Connecticut) Kennel Club Show, and there were 26 entries, judged by Stanley J. Halle. His Best of Breed was Carroll Bassett's *Ch. Toftwold Toffee* (Ch. Koffee Lad x Ch. Dalquest Derry Down). Best of Opposite Sex was *Ch. Portholme Bellarina of Dalquest* (Montime x Lassiebelle, bred by Mr. J. S. Bell and owned by Dalquest), who was almost nine years old at the time. Seven Borders completed their championships during the year, and two became Companion Dogs.

Ch. Toftwold Toffee also won the Specialty in 1965 over 26 dogs with John T. Marvin as judge. Best of Opposite Sex went to *Ch. Dalquest's Gillian* (Dalquest's Musket of Lent x Dalquest Kitterina) owned by Dalquest. Again, four champions for the year, and one Companion Dog.

The club shows for 1966, 1967 and 1968 were won by two Borders owned by Mrs. Webb. They were: *Eng. and Am. Ch. Deerstone Debrett* (Klein Otti x Deerstone Tinker Bell) and *Ch. Deerstone Tylview Dusty* (Eng. Ch. Deerstone Destiny x Tylview Shandy). In 1966, Mrs. Paul Silvernail gave Breed to the male, Opposite Sex to the bitch, with an entry of 20. The next year Louis J. Murr reversed the placings. The entry was 28. And in 1968, Mrs. Heywood Hartley put Debrett at the top, with Dusty Opposite, from an entry of 21.

The last Specialty Show of the '60s had an English judge for the first time. Mrs. B.S.T. Holmes, whose prefix Wharfholme appears frequently in pedigrees, had 31 dogs. Her choices were: Best of Breed, *Ch. Dandyhow Shady Lady* (also an English champion, Dandyhow Brussel Sprout x Eng. Ch. Dandyhow Soroya), owned by Kate (Webb) Seemann. Dalquest's *Ch. Dalquest Buddy MacTige* (Ch. Portholme Max Factor x Ch. Dalquest Smokey Tigress) was Best of Opposite Sex.

Dr. Pope died in late 1969 at the age of 86. He was one of the founders of the Border Terrier Club of America, and its president from 1949 to 1959. His Philabeg stock provided the foundation for many later kennels. Dr. Pope had a long and distinguished career in agronomy, and worked in the U.S. Department of Agriculture. In addition to his interest in Border Terriers, Dr. Pope bred Scottish Terriers.

During the decade's span, there were 73 Border Terriers who became Champions of Record, a respectable record given the relatively small number of the breed. Ten dogs gained C.D. obedience titles and one achieved the C.D.X. This was *Ch. Cinjola Toluidine Daisy* (Ch. Cinjola Little Red Recco's Son x Cinjola Toluidine Blue) bred by the Barkers and owned by Francis and Maxine Hoyne. New fanciers and breeders were attracted to the Border, such as Henry Mosle of *Town Hill* kennels and Margaret Pough, with *Bandersnatch.*

Border Terrier Club of America Specialty Show, 1969. L-R: Douglas Pfenninger (Ch. Town Hill's Sprinkle Star), Edmund Shaw (Bandersnatch Vorpal Blade), Mrs. Cottle (Town Hill Flopsey), Dale Gourlie (Ch. D.G.'s Wattie Irving of Dalquest), Mrs. Holmes, Mr. A. Bowers (Buckhurst Lark), Mrs. Bowers (Deerstone Dent), Henry Mosle (Falcliff Tantaliser), Mrs. Mosle (Birkfell Baroness Mischief),Holly Pfenninger (Coqo's Imp Clementine). Photo by Evelyn M. Shafer.

CHAPTER 3

The Border Terrier in the United States from 1970 to 1980

The decade of the '70s marked a great rise of interest in purebred dogs, including the Border Terrier. From 30 registrations in 1970, the number more than tripled by 1976.

The Border Terrier Club instituted two new awards in 1970. The first, the *Register of Merit* (ROM) recognizes the "Lifetime Achievements of outstanding Border Terrier sires and dams with A.K.C. offspring." There are three classifications: In males, the Gold ROM is awarded to dogs having 10 or more championship progeny; the Silver ROM, which signifies seven to nine champion get; and, the Bronze ROM, which signifies five or six champion get.

In bitches, the Gold originally meant seven or more champions produced; Silver, five or six; Bronze, three or four. In 1976, the requirements for dams were raised to eight for Gold; six or seven for the Silver; and four or five to win the Bronze.

The qualifications were raised again, effective January 1, 1991, with the additional requirement that ROM holders must have been bred to two different mates. For the Bronze ROM, dogs must have sired seven champions, bitches five; Silver ROM, dogs nine, bitches seven; Gold ROM, 12 for males, nine for females.

The other innovation was *Incentive Awards*: "To recognize sires and dams presently making an outstanding contribution to the breed." First offered in 1970, the award will be offered every third year. Certificates are presented to the owner and the breeder of each Border who has had the largest number of champion offspring during the preceding five years.

The 1970 Club Specialty Show was won by **Rose Bud of Lothian** (Ch. Portholme Macsleap of Dalquest x Town Hill Star of Lothian, bred by Mrs. James Pettigrew). Her owner was

Henry B. Mosle. Dalquest's *Hawkesburn Bison of Dalquest* was the Best of Opposite Sex. Judge for the 24 entries was Robert Hall from England, a longtime judge and breeder of the Deerstone Border Terriers. The following year, Rose Bud, now a champion, was Best of Opposite Sex to Marion duPont Scott's *Ch. Bull Run* (Ch. Koffee Lad x Bandersnatch Beamish, bred by L. Lewis). James Trullinger was the judge of 24 entries.

The fourth *Breed Booklet*, dated 1971 (although published in 1972), was edited by Marjory Van der Veer and Margaret Pough. Expanded to 143 pages, it included listings of officers, trophies, champions of record and obedience title holders, as well as breed information. There were photographs, major wins and pedigrees of all dogs who had won titles since the previous publication.

L-R: Ch. Bandersnatch Snark and Hanleycastle Roxana, 1971. Photo by John L. Ashbey.

Ch. Chief of Lothian, UDT, CG, TD, 1972.

Ch. Bandersnatch Snark, CD, CG, 1973. Photo by William P. Gilbert.

Am. and Eng. Ch. Final Honour, 1973. Photo by Anne Roslin Williams.

Ch. Shuttle, Gold ROM, 1975. Photo by William P. Gilbert.

John T. Marvin contributed an article, "The Border Terrier, Past and Present," in which he stressed the need for keeping the Border's appearance and temperament unchanged: "[I]t should always be remembered that each breed was developed with a specific purpose in mind and to modify basic characteristics, that have taken years to develop, for the mere sake of whim or beauty, will eventually destroy the very reason for the breed's existence."

English breeder, Felicity Marchant, writing on "The Qualities Required in a Working Border Terrier," emphasized the same points, remarking: "Each point of the Standard of the Breed plays a vital part. Any deviations caused by fad or fancy of the show ring will weaken working ability. This has been the sad fate of many fashionable breeds of terriers."

Co-Editor Margaret Pough provided a detailed account of "Coat Color Genetics in Border Terriers," which was complemented by Hester Garnett-Orme's, "Coat Colour — From Puppy to Adult."

Border owners became more and more involved with training and working their dogs. Nancy Hughes's *Ch. Chief of Lothian* (Wharfholme Whipperin x Ch. Rose Bud of Lothian, bred by Mrs. J. Pettigrew) was the star performer. After winning C.D. and C.D.X. titles, the red-grizzle went on to become the breed's first Tracking Dog and Utility Dog. He also held an American Working Terrier Association Certificate of Gameness (CG), acquired in 1974. In addition, Chief won the 1972 Club Specialty over an entry of 33, with Percy Roberts judging. David V. Kline's import, *Ch. Rhosmerholme Belinda* (Eng. Ch. Ribbleside Falcliff Trident x Rhosmerholme Agustine, bred by E. Garnett) was Best of Opposite Sex. The Specialty moved to Woodstock, Vermont, where it remained for many years.

In 1971, the American Working Terrier Association was founded by Patricia A. Lent. Its stated purpose is "to encourage and promote...the breeding, hunting, and ownership of terriers of size, conformation, and character to perform as...working terriers." Margaret Pough's home-bred *Ch. Bandersnatch Snark, CD* (Ch. Espresso x Ch. Bandersnatch Brillig CD) was the first Border Terrier to gain a CG in 1972. The dog had completed his championship the previous year, including a Group placement — a fine example of the breed's ability to maintain its working heritage as well as to perform in the show ring.

The year 1972 witnessed another very important first in the breed: Dale Gourlie was the proud owner of **Ch. D.G.'s Wattie Irving of Dalquest,** the first Border Terrier to win the Terrier Group. Bred by Dalquest, Wattie was sired by Ch. Portholme Macsleap of Dalquest, ROM, out of Dalquest Kitterina. Mr. Gourlie had joined the Club in 1967 and later became a board member and president. A talented artist, he wrote and illustrated *Visual Discussion of the Border Terrier,* and many other art works for the club. His kennel name was *Cheviot,* and he was responsible in large part for the interest in Border Terriers on the West Coast. His early death in 1978 was a great loss.

The winner of the 1973 Specialty was Kate J. Seemann's **Monty of Essenhigh,** an import bred by Mrs. M.J. Howden (Eng. Ch. Yak Bob x Essenhigh Patricia). **Ch. Rhosmerholme Belinda** was again awarded Best of Opposite Sex by British judge Stanley Dangerfield, who drew 37 entries.

An overseas judge was again the club's choice for its 1974 show, with 58 dogs entered — the largest number so far. W. Ronald Irving came from Scotland, and his Best of Breed was **Eng. and Am. Ch. Final Honour** (Eng. Ch. Wharfholme Warrant x Miss Georgina, bred by Mrs. P. Perry) owned by Nancy Hughes and David V. Kline. Best of Opposite Sex was Dalquest Kennels' **Chevinor Maria of Dalquest**; she finished her championship that year. She was bred in England by A.H. Beardwood (Eng. Ch. Duttonlea Mr. Softy x Chevinor Remarvic).

By 1975, there were more than 100 members of the BTCA, and the Specialty had 42 entries. Robert Hall came from England to judge the show for the second time. His pick was **Chevinor Rojane,** a bitch imported by Wayne Moldovan (again, bred by Mr. Beardwood; Eng. Ch. Duttonlea Mr. Softy x Chevinor Renoble). Mr. Hall's critique included some of the following comments on his winner: "Typical blue and tan, correct flat skull with muzzle in correct proportion... well laid shoulders... liked her Border expression and overall balance." Of **Ch. Llanishen Senator,** Best of Opposite Sex, he wrote: "very stylish...good skull...correct in stifle." Owned by Dr. H.V. Mishler, the dog was bred in England by D. Wiseman (Llanishen Ludovic x Hanleycastle Julie). Mr. Hall also remarked that, allowing for the male and female differences, the Borders were "similar in type." His critiques were particularly interesting, as Mr. Hall had been judging the breed for more than 25 years, and his Deerstone prefix appears in many U.S. pedigrees.

The Gold Register of Merit dam, **Ch. Dalquest Dare's Dancer**, died in 1975 after a long and productive career of more than 17 years. She was owned by *Cinjola Kennels* and bred by Dalquest. In 1975, Marion duPont Scott's **Ch. Shuttle** (Ch. Bull Run x Katie) was the first bitch to win the Terrier Group.

In 1976, Judge Mary Jane Ellis wrote a short general critique of the Specialty entry of 45, remarking that the Border is "one of the few breeds that remain unspoiled...May I suggest that the breed could stray from being a true working terrier if oversprung ribs and short backs become too prevalent." She made no individual comments on the winners. **Ch. Dalquest Border Lord** (Dalquest MacDandyhow Tarek x Ch. Chevinor Maria of Dalquest, bred by Dalquest and owned by C.J. Atkins and J.L. Ormiston) was Best of Breed, and Best of Opposite Sex was **Ch. Borderseal Bessie**, Robert Naun's English-bred bitch (Eng. Ch. Clipstone Guardsman x Borderseal Chuc Wuca, bred by B. Dark).

In 1977, imported Borders took Specialty honors under British judge Frank Jackson, of the *Clipstone* name. From his 47 Terriers he selected Kate Seemann's imported **Ch. Workmore Waggoner WC**, who went on to win the Specialty for five consecutive years, surely a record in any breed. The dog also held an English championship. Sired by Coppins Well Dandy Boy out of Eng. Ch. Workmore Rascal, his breeder was Mrs. C. Walker.

Mr. Jackson's Best of Opposite Sex was Patricia Quinn's **Avim Dainty Girl**, (later champion) also from England (Solway Cawfields Duke x Avim Gundi, bred by A. Mountain). Tuppence, as she was called, won her Working Certificate and CG that year. The following year she became a Canadian champion.

The breed's first Obedience Champion was a dog called **Pete U.D.**, ancestry unknown, with an Indefinite Listing Privilege as a Border Terrier. Owned by Floyd E. Timmons, Detroit, Michigan, Pete won his title in 1978.

The 1978 *Breed Book* of 208 pages was edited by Margaret B. Pough and dedicated to Marjory L. Van der Veer and Margery B. Harvey. The dedication said in part: "Dalquest Borders are found country-wide as champions and beloved pets. In recognition of what the breed in this country owes to them, this breed book is dedicated to the Ladies of Dalquest."

Memorials were written to Henry B. Mosle, who died in 1978. He had been a club member since 1964 and served in various offices, including the presidency. His *Town Hill* kennel contributed much to the breed, and Mr. Mosle's help as liaison with the American Kennel Club was invaluable.

Tribute was also paid to the late Dale Gourlie, whose many contributions to the club have been cited earlier.

The book gave updates on officers, trophies, champions and obedience winners, as well as other statistics. Special features included Miss Van der Veer's, "The Dalquest Story," giving its history from the first Border Terrier acquired, **Ch. Philabeg Red Bet** in 1947, to the date of writing. Damara Bolté provided a look at "The Borders of Montpelier." "Van" also delved into her enormous files to produce "The Border Terrier Club of America," a history from which much of the information in this book has been taken.

Ch. Workmore Waggoner won the 1978 show, with James Reynolds awarding Opposite Sex to **Ch. Nonstop**, owned by Jane Lodge and Marion duPont Scott, the latter the breeder (Ch. Rob Roy's Buckler x Ch. Shuttle). There were 40 entries. In 1979, Waggoner took the Specialty for the third time — this time from an entry of more than 79 dogs. Best of Opposite Sex was Nancy Hughes's **Lothlorien Final Step**, who became a champion the following year (Ch. Brockett Hurdle CD CG x Ch. Trail's End Peaceful Bree CDX CG WC HC, bred by JoAnn Frier). The judge was Mrs. M. Aspinwall from England, of *Farmway* note, a long-time breeder and judge.

And so another eventful decade ended with many new owners and breeders rapidly increasing show entries and greater interest in the working ability of the Border Terrier. Next are some brief sketches of a few of the breeders of the 1970s, many of whom began their kennels in the '60s. Some are active at the time of writing (1992) and are listed alphabetically by kennel names.

Ch. Oldstone Ragrug, 1979. Photo by William P. Gilbert.

The 1974 BTCA Specialty Show. L-R: Jane and Henry Mosle, Marjorie Van der Veer, Judge W. Ronald Irving. Photo courtesy of Nancy Hughes.

Bandersnatch is the kennel name of Margaret and Harvey Pough, of Ithaca, New York. Mrs. Pough bought her first Border, *Mex. Ch. Dalquest Jody of Town Hill*, from Dalquest in 1963. At that time, Mrs. Pough lived in New York City, and wanted "a dog small enough for a city apartment, and tough enough to go and enjoy the country with me."

Jody's first litter, sired by Ch. Portholme Macsleap of Dalquest, was whelped in 1965. One of the offspring, *Bandersnatch Brillig, CD*, became both an American and a Mexican title holder.

Since then, the Borders have been bred, shown and worked by Mrs. Pough — a tradition carried on by her daughter Amanda. Mrs.Pough has headed the club's Genetics Committee and has edited or co-edited the year books since 1971. In 1992, Mrs. Pough was elected president of the BTCA.

The **Barrister Kennels** (Formerly Ariel) is the prefix of Mr. and Mrs. Kenneth Klothen of Swarthmore, Pennsylvania. It was established in 1974 with the acquisition of *Ch. Little Fir Gremlin of Ariel* (Gold ROM, sired by Eng. and Am. Ch. Final Honour x Ch. Little Fir Autumngold, bred by David V. Kline). Gremlin sired a litter out of *Ch. Express*, owned by Carol Sowders, which included *Ch. Ketka Barrister's Speed Trap*. Among other winners from this kennel were *Ch. Ariel's Little Fir Bridgett* and *Ch. Barrister's Buckeye*.

Although Canada is somewhat beyond the scope of this book, **Birkfell** should be included. This is the prefix of C.M. June Monaghan of British Columbia. She had grown up with Borders in England and, after coming to Canada, she acquired *Birkfell Emma* in 1954. Later, several dogs were imported from England and the United States, and many of Mrs. Monaghan's Borders appear in American pedigrees. Her *Birkfell Bobber Burrills* was both an American and Canadian champion (Can. Ch. Hawkesburn Badger x Can. and Am. Ch. Deerstone Damsel). Although no longer active in showing and breeding, Mrs. Monaghan still enjoys her dogs as companions.

California fanciers Betty Green and Jacqueline Appel of Bakersfield acquired their first Border in 1967 and bred their first litter in 1971. They took the kennel name **Brigatyne**. The import *Ch. Hanleycastle Wasp* (Coundon Tribesman x

Hanleycastle Wee Willow) was their foundation bitch. Her first litter was sired by Ch. Bandersnatch Vorpal Blade (Ch. Dalquest Buddy MacTige x Ch. Bandersnatch Brillig, CD). All of the puppies from this first litter were named after novels by Sir Walter Scott, including *Ch. Brigatyne Guy Mannering*.

Delores Snead, Virginia Beach, Virginia, was the owner of **Coastland Kennel**. In 1975, she acquired her first Border, *Ch. Little Fir Honour Guard* (Eng. and Am. Ch. Final Honour x Rob Roy's Red Fox, bred by L. and E. Hammett). This dog was the sire of Coastland's first litter in 1981, out of *Ch. Ketka Lorelei* (Ch. Ketka Swashbuckler CG x Ch. Ketka Gopher Broke CG, bred by C. Sowders), which included *Ch. Coastland's Eddie's Honour*.

Patricia Quinn, Silverhill, Alabama, bought her first of the breed in 1974 and bred her first litter in 1976. Her kennel is called **Foxley**. Her first import was *Avim Dainty Girl*, who became a champion in America, Canada and Bermuda. Sired by Solway Cawfields Duke out of Avim Gundi, "Tuppence," as she was called, was the first Border Terrier to win a Working Certificate, and by working a fox. She also won a CG.

Mrs. Quinn has been active in the breed club, serving as secretary and as editor of *The Borderline*. In addition to campaigning her dogs in the show ring, she is especially interested in the working aspect of the breed and is an official American Working Terrier Association judge.

Gizella Szilagyi, **Greenbriar Kennel**, of Middleburg Heights, Ohio, acquired her first Border in 1978. This was *Bandersnatch Jubjub Bird*, bred by H. and M. Pough (Ch. Bandersnatch Snark, CDX x Ch. Bandersnatch Border in Blue). "Blue Jeans" (her call name) went on to become a champion in both this country and Canada, and she earned CDX, CG and Certified Therapy Dog. The late Miss Szilagyi's dogs were shown in conformation and Working Trials.

Jean Sedlak, of **Kaldes Borders**, Duluth, Minnesota, is interested in working and obedience, as well as conformation. In 1976, she bought her first bitch from Betsy Finley, *Ch. Woodlawn's Star Border, CD* (Ch. Little Fir Kirksman x Ch. Dalquest Rebeca of Woodlawn ROM). "Mandy," as she's called, became the dam of three litters, and her 1980 daughter, *Am. and Can. Ch. Kaldes Katrina, CG*, sired by Ch. Ketka Swashbuckler, produced well for Kaldes.

Ch. Trails End Peaceful Bree, UD, CG, WC, HC with offspring. Photo courtesy of N. Hiscock.

Ch. Stonecroft Tristan, CG, 1979.

Ch. Oldstone Brampton Sweet. Photo by Diane Pearce.

Carol Sowders' **Ketka Kennels**, Galien, Michigan, began in 1974 with the purchase of *Dalquest Ketka's Kritter, CD* (Dalquest MacDandyhow Tarek x Ch. Dalquest Abbe Gale). In 1976, Miss Sowders bought *Ch. Little Fir Rob Roy's Robin* (Ch. Farmway Dandyhow Likely Lad x Rob Roy's Red Fox, bred by L. Hammett). Robin, when bred to Ch. Rob Roy's Buckler, produced the noted Gold ROM sire, *Ch. Ketka Swashbuckler* (co-owner Helen Hudson). Ketka has had many champions, among which are *Ch. Ketka Short Circuit, Ch. Ketka Kiwi*, and *Ch. Ketka Qwik Charge of Dalfox*.

The Borders owned by Janis Leventhal of Mamaroneck, New York, demonstrate the versatility of the breed. Mrs. Leventhal acquired her first in 1977 — a year-old import *Ch. Malbrant Medina, CDX* (Roserll Claudio x Malbrant Bardot, bred by Mrs. D. K. Davies). "Charity," as she was called, lived to the fine old age of 15. She and her daughter *Ch. Faith, CDX* (sired by Ch. Lothlorien Jollymuff Bumper), who is now retired at age 13, visited nursing homes, played fly-ball and appeared on television, among other activities. Continuing the tradition, *Ch. George, CD* (Charity's son by Ch. Oldstone Ragrug) does therapy work by visiting schools and hospitals.

JoAnn Frier-Murza, Crosswicks, New Jersey, is the owner of **Lothlorien Working Terriers**, and the emphasis is indeed on *working*. Her first Border, and the foundation of her kennel, was *Ch. Trail's End Peaceful Bree UD, WC, CG, HC* and *Gold ROM*. She was bred by Nancy Hughes (Eng. and Am. Ch. Final Honour x Eng. and Am. Ch. Workmore Brackon) and provided original stock for many other Border kennels. Bree died in 1990. Eighteen litters have come from this kennel.

Ch. Todfield Truffle. Photo by William P. Gilbert.

Ch. Edenbrae Dusky Maiden with two future champions.

Ch. Ketka Qwik Charge of Dalfox.

The owner writes: "...what sets the Border apart from most other breeds. They are DOGS, they are not ornamental, they are not docked, cropped or fussed with, they just exist for what dogs exist for — to please their owners and improve their lives with their companionship."

Oldstone, the kennel name of Ruth Ann and Robert Naun of Mahopac, New York, came into being in 1972. The Nauns' first two Borders were imports: *Ch. Borderseal Bessie* (Eng. Ch. Clipstone Guardsman x Borderseal Chuc Wuca, bred by B. Dark) and English-bred *Scotland Buddy* (Eng. Ch. Handy Andy x Rulewater Holly), who was the sire of Bessie's first litter.

Since that time, almost 60 litters have been whelped at Oldstone, and the owners have bred, owned or co-owned more than 30 champions. Their *Ch. Oldstone Ragrug* (Bessie's offspring by Ch. Dandyhow Bertie Bassatt) holds the Gold ROM.

The Nauns have been active in the Border Terrier Club of America: Mr. Naun served as president and Mrs. Naun as the club delegate to the AKC. Both the Nauns are licensed to judge Borders.

Dr. Norman W. Crisp (New Hampshire) and his family bought their first Border from Dalquest in 1968. This dog, *Ch. Dalquest Macsleap's How Dandy* (Ch. Portholme Macsleap of Dalquest x Ch. Dandyhow Schnapps of Dalquest), was shown by Elizabeth Crisp as a junior handler. The Crisps have been loyal supporters of the breed for many years. At present, Elizabeth Crisp Blake, of Davis, California, is the owner of *Ch. Ryswick Remember Me, ROM* (Ch. Ryswick Ranger x Ryswick Return of Post, bred by A. P. Willis) and is actively showing and breeding. In 1989, Mrs. Blake took over the breed column in the AKC *Gazette* from Miss Van der Veer, who had written it since the club's acceptance.

Red Eft, Mrs. Nancy Hiscock's prefix, is located in Porter Corners, New York. The first dog, *Ch. Lothlorien's Easy Strider* (Ch. Little Fir Gremlin of Ariel x Ch. Trails End Peaceful Bree, bred by Jo Ann Frier), was acquired in 1977. Also a Canadian champion, he held UD, WC and CG titles. Mrs. Hiscock is interested in the working aspects of the breed as well as the show ring.

Am. and Can. Ch. Kaldes Katrina, CG. Photo by William P. Gilbert.

Stonecroft is the kennel of Jean Oswell Clark, of Weare, New Hampshire. Her first Border came from the kennel of Henry Mosle in 1970. This was *Town Hill Smoke Ring* (Eng. and Am. Ch. Falcliff Tantaliser x Can. Ch. Birkfell Baroness Mischief). In 1976, Mrs. Clark imported and finished *Ch. Farmway Miss Feather* (Eng. Ch. Farmway Fine Feather x Farmway Marsham Wren, bred by M. Aspinwall). To date, Mrs. Clark has made up eight champions, all owner-handled and four of which she bred. In addition, several of her dogs hold working titles.

David V. Kline, Manassas, Virginia, became involved in the breed in 1970 with the acquisition of the English imports, *Ch. Rhosmerholme Belinda* (Eng. Ch. Ribbleside Falcliff Trident x Rhosmerholme Agustine, bred by Mrs. E. Garnett) and *Ch. Falcliff Target* (Eng. Ch. Falcliff Topper x Deerstone Daybreak, bred by Mr. E. Mawson). All of this kennel's Terriers are descended from this foundation pair. First established as Little Fir, the kennel later took the prefix **Todfield**. Mr. Kline is the only United States breeder to have bred three Gold ROM sires:

Ch. Little Fir Gremlin of Ariel, Ch. Little Fir Kirksman and *Ch. Todfield Trafalgar Square.* The top-winning Best in the BTCA Specialty Sweepstakes trophy was retired by this kennel with three dogs: *Ch. Little Fir Honour Guard, Ch. Little Fir Gremlin of Ariel* and *Ch. Todfield Trafalgar Square.* Mr. Kline was active on the BTCA Board in the '70s, serving as vice-president and as editor of *The Borderline.* He is an AKC-licensed judge of Borders.

Nancy J. Hughes' **Trails End Kennels,** West Chicago, Illinois, was established in 1969 with the breed's first UDT champion, *Chief of Lothian* (Wharfholm Whipperin x Ch. Rose Bud of Lothian, bred by Mrs. J. Pettigrew). Mrs. Hughes has imported noted winners, including *Eng. and Am. Ch. Workmore Brackon, Ch. Wharfholme Top Hostess, Eng. and Am. Ch. Final Honour* (co-owned with D.V. Kline), *Ch. Dandyhow Herdsman* (later owned by Kris Blake) and *Ch. Duttonlea Autocrat of Dandyhow.* The latter was the all-time top sire with more than 40 champion get. In addition, Trails End has produced many Borders holding obedience, working and conformation titles under its own name.

Hazel Wichman and her daughter Jennifer call their kennel **von Hasselwick**. Their first Border, *Ch. Sandy MacGregor V. Hasselwick, CD,* "entered our lives Saturday, December 21, 1976 and is still alive at this time." They live in Morris Plains, New Jersey. Sandy was bred by F.A. Mettler (Farmway Sandling x Clarfar Tawny of Rema) and also has a Canadian CD. The dogs of von Hasselwick are both show and obedience trained and have participated in various other activities.

Betsy Finley, of Shoreview, Minnesota, started her **Woodlawn Kennels** in 1975, and her stock has provided the foundation for many others. Her first Border Terrier was *Am. and Can. Ch. Dalquest Rebeca of Woodlawn,* Gold ROM (Deerstone Ryak of Dalquest x Dalquest Teri), bred by Dalquest. Her first stud dog, *Ch. Little Fir Kirksman* (Ch. Llanishen Senator x Ch. Little Fir Autumngold, bred by D. V. Kline) was also a Gold ROM. Since then Mrs. Finley has been the breeder, or co-breeder, of more than 100 champions — in addition to 13 imports who won their titles. Her import, *Ch. Edenbrae Dusky Maiden* (Elandmead Prospect x Tarka May Princess, bred by Miss M. Edgar), co-owned with M. Pickford was also a Gold ROM dam. She died at the age of 15.

Ch. Coastland's Eddie's Honour and Coastland's Ketka Madonna.

CHAPTER 4

The Border Terrier After 1980

The year 1980 marked an important event for the Border Terrier Club of America. After several years of effort, it became a member of the American Kennel Club, and its first delegate, elected in 1981, was Ruth Ann Naun, who continues to hold the position. As stated previously, the AKC had accepted the official Standard of the Breed 30 years earlier, and the Standard has remained unchanged.

There were 59 Borders for Judge Louis Auslander at the 1980 Specialty, with *Ch. Workmore Waggoner* again the winner, and *Ch. Nonstop* repeating her 1978 Best of Opposite Sex win.

By 1981, there were 224 club members, and 249 Borders registered with the AKC. Honors at the Specialty went to two Borders owned by Kate Seemann, as Waggoner won for the fifth time and was retired. His daughter, out of Ch. Redridge Russet, *Ch. Shelburn Ragus*, was BOS. The judge was Dr. Lee Huggins.

Marjory L. Van der Veer resigned in 1982 from the office of club secretary, a post she had held since the club's beginning. Without "Van's" efforts and determination, the breed in this country might well not have survived. We all owe "Van" and her partner Margery Harvey immeasurable thanks.

Kate Irving traveled from the United Kingdom to judge the 1982 show. Seventy-one entries were topped by Nancy Hughes's import, *Ch. Duttonlea Autocrat of Dandyhow* (Dandyhow Grenadier x Ribbleside Morning Dew, bred by W. Wrigley). Mrs. Hughes had the pleasure of seeing her home-bred *Trails End Good Gracious* win Best of Opposite Sex. Her sire was the day's winner and her dam was Eng. Ch. Dandyhow Forget-Me-Not.

The BTCA's Silver Jubilee, held in 1983, had a large entry of 97 dogs, with Clifford W. Thompson Jr. as judge. Again, the winner was *Ch. Duttonlea Autocrat of Dandyhow*, and the Best of Opposite Sex went to *Ch. Cotswold Poppy* (Ch. Solo x Ch. Llanishen Sophia, bred by R.C. Morgan). Her owners were B. Hohn and E. Levy Jr.

Sadly, Marion duPont Scott died in 1983. Mrs. Scott, one of the true pillars of the breed in the United States, provided tremendous financial support to the club with her typical modesty. Her memory is continued by the club with the annual Rally at her home, Montpelier, near Orange, Virginia. The Terriers were taken on by Damara Bolté of Leesburg, Virginia, who has continued to show and breed.

The *Sixth Breed Book* issued by the BTCA in 1983 was edited by Margaret B. Pough. Carefully researched and accurate, it listed every possible fact and figure dealing with Borders. There were no articles, but every title-holding dog was listed and illustrated, with major wins and pedigrees given. Also included were complete rosters of officers, trophies, statistics from the American Working Terrier Association, Register of Merit — nothing was omitted, and as a source book for the breed it is invaluable.

The year 1984 was a very busy year. Fred G. Ferris judged the Specialty of 82 entries. His choices were: Best of Breed, *Ch. Starcyl March On*, owned by Kate Seemann (Foxhill Footstep out of Starcyl Way Ahead,bred in England by Mr. and Mrs. J. McCrystals): Best of Opposite Sex, B. and L. Anthony's *Ch. Seabrook Galadiel*, a home-bred bitch by Ch. Solo x Ch. Concorde. Mr. Ferris commented on his breed winner: "[H]e possessed many fine qualities and no major faults ... proper in size, moving well with drive and reach." Mr. Ferris felt that the overall quality of Borders had improved but cautioned: "Don't lose proper bone or become overrefined in heads...This is a true working terrier, so be more critical of your own stock for the betterment of the breed... don't stylize or popularize this friendly, game as they come, companion."

By 1985, there were 327 members of BTCA. Peter Thompson (Thoraldby Borders) came from England to judge the record-breaking entry of 102 at the Specialty. Best of Breed was *Ch. Traveler of Foxley*, bred by Patricia Quinn and owned by Barbara Kemp (Br. Ch. Ashbrae Jaffa x Ch. Thoraldby Magic Moment CG). The judge's comments: "My idea of a Border. Good head and eye with well shaped ears... Best mover of the day." Of the entry in general: "My big criticism was overweight ... With being overweight this makes their fronts go wide. Also scissors had been used which should be frowned upon." Best of Opposite Sex was *Foxley's Smash* (Ch. Duttonlea Autocrat of Dandyhow x Ch. Thoraldby Magic Chip) owned by J. Gilman and bred by Mrs. Quinn.

First held in 1985, the Border Rally at Montpelier has since become an annual event. It is held in April, as close in date as possible to that of the club's first Sanctioned Match of 1957. This was also the birthday of Marion duPont Scott's favorite Border, Wallace. Montpelier, once the home of James Madison, now belongs to the National Trust and is a most interesting and historic estate.

Ch. Solo, 1981. Photo by William P. Gilbert.

Ch. Woodbine Woodland Wonder, CDX, CG, 1982.

The Rally owes its success to the untiring efforts of Mr. and Mrs. Edwin Levy Jr. who have organized and managed this event every year. The Rally is held, appropriately, on the private racecourse for steeplechasing. It is a day designed to show the various capabilities of the Border Terrier, with conformation, obedience, racing, working and other events. It's fun for all — spectators, owners and, of course, the dogs.

In 1984, the Border Terrier Club published its *Breed Book Update, 1983 - 1985* edited by Margaret Pough. Like its immediate predecessor, it contains no articles, but is a complete record of the period covered. It lists all champions, obedience and working titles, with photos, major wins and pedigrees. Also included are lists of officers, trophies and other pertinent information. It has an index, with references to the previous breed book — an enormously useful addition.

Ch. Duttonlea Autocrat of Dandyhow, 1982. Photo by William P. Gilbert.

Ch. Seabrook Galadiel, 1983. Photo by Earl Graham.

Ch. Trails End Fur Trapper, 1983. Photo by K. Blake.

1984 Specialty Show, Stud Dog Class. L-R: Ch. Ketka's Wicket, Ch. Ketka Fizzgig, Ch. Seabrook Spriggan. Photo by William P. Gilbert.

Ch. Jocasta Just Sara, 1984. Photo by Missy Yuhl.

Ch. Barrister's Just Because, CDX, 1984. Photo by Klein.

In March 1986, an additional National Specialty Show was held in Bakersfield, California. David V. Kline judged the 66 entries, and his Best of Breed was *Ch. Trails End Barney*, owned by T. Yuill (Ch. Duttonlea Autocrat of Dandyhow x Eng. Ch. Dandyhow Forget-Me-Not, bred by N. Hughes). Best of Opposite Sex was *Ch. Jocasta Just Sara* (Ch. Standby x BB's Busybody), bred and co-owned by D. Blake and L. Tofflemire.

The Second Annual Rally was held at Montpelier with the usual large attendance. Also, the regularly scheduled National Specialty was held in Vermont and judged by Marilyn Drewes. From an entry of 104, she selected *Ch. Duttonlea Autocrat of Dandyhow* for his third win of the Specialty. A granddaughter of his, *Ch. Glenburnie's Becky Thatcher* (Ch. Trails End Barney x Woodlawns Vixen O'Glenburnie), owned by N. Hughes and T. Beverly was Best of Opposite Sex.

Popularity of the Border has continued to increase. In the late 1980s, many more breeders entered the scene, some to stay, others to drop out (true of any breed). At the end of 1992, there were breeders in nearly every state, including Alaska. Interest in trials, obedience and the sports of tracking and agility was also on the upswing.

Additional breed books were published, compiled and edited by Margaret Pough. The 1991 issue listed all titled holders through 1987 — a monumental task, as it included lists of trophy winners, the 1987 Specialty Show winners, Group Placements, Register of Merit, the 56 champions made

Ch. Royal Oaks Gilda Ratter, CG, 1985. Photo by Callea.

up that year, plus obedience titles. This last includes three UDs and one TDX. Photographs and pedigrees of the 1987 winners made up the bulk of this comprehensive work.

It would be difficult, indeed impossible, to discuss in detail all those breeders and fanciers not previously mentioned who have done so much for the Border Terrier. A few representative kennels of the 1980s and 1990s are given here, alphabetically by the owner's name.

Julianne and Geoffrey Amidon of Hudson, Florida, acquired their first Border Terrier in 1977. Since then, their **Woodbine Kennel** has produced several champions, all owner-handled. In addition, their dogs have held four CDs, one CDX and five CGs. "We are interested in many areas, showing, obedience, and working," says Mrs. Amidon.

Barbara Anthony, and her daughter Leslie Anthony Jaseph, of Seabrook, Maryland, use the prefix **Seabrook**. Since owning their first Border, the Anthonys have bred a number of winning dogs, notably *Ch. Seabrook Spriggan Gold ROM* (Ch. Ketka's Barrister's Speed Trap x Ch. Concorde) and *Ch. Seabrook Galadiel* (Ch. Solo x Ch. Concorde), winner of a third place in the Terrier Group at the AKC Centennial Show in 1983.

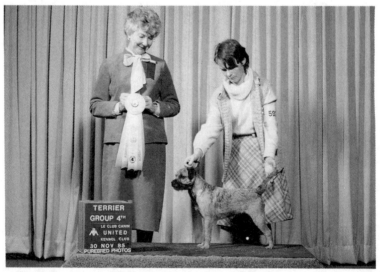

Can. and Am. Ch. Jansim Lothlorien Pepper, CG, Can. CD, 1985. Photo by Purebred Photos.

Ch. Luvemur's First Edition, CD, CG, 1985. Photo by Lloyd W. Olson.

Ch. Herdsman of Dandyhow, CG, 1985. Photo by Kris Blake.

*Ch. Woodlawn's
Dusky Gentleman,
ROM, 1986.*

*Ch. Saucy Debutante of
But'N Ben, CG, with
litter, 1986.*

Ch. Glenburnie's Becky Thatcher, 1986. Photo by Ashbey.

Ch. Todfield Trinket, 1987. Photo by Earl Graham.

Ch. Royal Oaks Scrap of Wolfsbane, 1987. Photo by Callea.

Norm Barker, **Barker Borders,** formerly a breeder of Great Danes, is now a Terrier enthusiast. He saw his first specimen in Scotland in 1982. He comments that he finds "Borders very rewarding. Extremely intelligent."

Michael and Elaine Benkert are from Lake Zurich, Illinois, and their kennel name is **Tin Whistle.** Of their current six adult Borders, two are champions and one, *Ch. Tin Whistle Tiggy-Winkle* (Ch. Herdsman of Dandyhow x Bani Berwick-Upon-Tweed), holds a CD. Mrs. Benkert is an accomplished artist and has illustrated both the national publication, *The Borderline,* and the Great Lakes Club's newsletter.

From Gresham, Oregon, comes Debra Janes Blake with the kennel name **Jocasta.** Her first Border was *Ch. Standby* (Ch. Rob Roy's Buckler x Ch. Shuttle, bred by Mrs. Scott), and he was the foundation sire of her kennel.

Kris Blake's **Saga Hill** is located in Maple Plain, Minnesota. Many of her dogs stem from Nancy Hughes's Trails End stock. The first of Mrs. Blake's many home-bred champions was *Saga Hill's Whistlin' Dixie* (Ch. Trails End Fur Trapper x Ch. Woodlawns Angel Dusk) whelped in 1984. A current star is the import, *Ch. Nettleby Nighthawk, WC, CG* (Eng. Ch. Lyddington Lets Go x Blaiseen Souvenir). Mrs. Blake is an expert photographer, and several of her excellent works illustrate this book.

Am. and Can. Ch. Von Hasselwick Gamekeeper. Am. and Can. CD, CG and therapy dog, 1988.

Ch. Ryswick Remember Me, 1988. Photo by Chuck Tatham.

Therapy dog and movie star (**Running on Empty**) *Ch. Sandy MacGregor. Am. and Can. CG, CD, 1988.*

Terri D. Beverly, Deltona, Florida, started her **Bever Lea Border Terriers** in 1982, acquiring *Ch. Barrister's Just Because CDX, CG* (Ch. Ketka's Barrister's Speed Trap x Barrister's Case Precedent, bred by K. and E. Klothen). Mrs. Beverly states: "Since all our dogs are house pets we have a limited breeding program, therefore we have had only eight litters." From them have come 14 title holders, three CDs, two CDXs and one CG. Co-owned with Linda Townsend, *Ch. Bever Lea Bewitching Brew, CD,* was Best of Winners at the 1991 Specialty (Ch. Krispin Calirose Bentley x Ch. Bever Lea Polly Pureheart).

Sandy Briggs of Claremont, Ontario, has the Canadian-registered kennel name of **Wimberway.** Her Borders have come from both the United States and England, and many hold both Canadian and U.S. championships. Wimberway dogs take part in obedience and Terrier trials, the latter under consideration by the Canadian Kennel Club as an official event. Mrs. Briggs is a Canadian obedience judge and a director of the CKC.

State College, Pennsylvania, is the home of **Krispin Border Terriers**, owned by Dail P. Corl. Her interest arose when she was on a trip to Scotland to buy Clydesdale horses. Her *Ch. Steephollow Little Nell* was Best of Breed at the 1989 Specialty (Ch. Traveler of Foxley x Ch. Duttonlea Genie, bred by Barbara Kemp). Mrs. Corl's *Ch. Woodlawns Dusky Gentleman* (Ch. Foxley Bright Forecast x Ch. Woodlawn's Cinnamon Twist, bred by S. J. O'Hair and M. Finley) holds the Gold Register of Merit award and has sired many winners.

Ch. Ryswick Remember Me, 1988. Photo by Tatham.

Ch. Steephollow Little Nell, 1989. Photo by Booth.

Am. and Can. Ch. Behm Allegretto, 1989.

L-R: Steephollow Firefly, Ch. Traveler of Foxley, Ch. Duttonlea Genie, 1990. Photo by E. Watkins.

Am. and Can. Ch. Jansim PC Sage, CG, 1989.

L-R: Towzie Tyke Nessie, CD, CG, WCh, ROM, Ch. Towzie Tyke Tweedle-Dee, CD, CG, WCh, Ch.Cotswold Dee Dee, CD, CG, WCh, 1989.

1989. The day Hurricane Hugo hit halfway through judging. L-R: Elizabeth Crisp Blake with Ch. Ryswick Remember me, Marjorie Van der Veer (judge), Dr. Norman V. Crisp with Ch. Dykeside Kristina. Photo by Ashbey.

Ch. Royal Oaks Rhatt Butler, CG, 1989. Photo by Bruni.

Tyrian Red Alert, 1990.

L-R: Ch. Dandyhow Top Notch and Ch. Oldstone Brass Ring.

Sandy MacGregor at 13 with two young friends.

Ch. Rockferry Bomber Boy, 1990.

Royal Oaks is owned by Eric and Ardis Dahlstrom of Hydesville, California. In 1985, their *Royal Oaks Gilda Ratter, CG* (Otter B Sumpthin Special x Bubblin Brown Sugar, bred by B. And R. Ellis Jr.) produced their first litter, sired by Ch. Duttonlea Autocrat of Dandyhow. To date Royal Oaks has produced 10 champions, some of which have obedience degrees. The Dahlstroms are very active in Terrier trials, and state: "We won't breed a dog or bitch that cannot demonstrate hunting abilities." They add that a good sense of humor is needed to train Borders.

Another enthusiast for the working ability of the Border Terrier is Carolyn Dostal of Chicago, Illinois, with the **Rycar** kennel name. She entered the sport in the early 1980s, and presently owns three Borders, who hold obedience degrees as well as CG and TT certificates. They participate in obedience as well as agility, and Mrs. Dostal, a member of the U.S. Dog Agility Association, has contributed information and photos on that sport for this book.

Another Canadian kennel is **Jansim** of Ste. Madeleine, Quebec, belonging to Chris and Pam Dyer. Since their entrance into the fancy in 1980, the Dyers' dogs have won three U.S. championships and 10 Canadian, as well as eight CGs, two WCs and a number of obedience titles. Both Dyers are American Working Terrier judges, and Mrs. Dyer has been involved with the North American Border Terrier Welfare since it began in 1989. These breeders insist on sound temperament and working ability and characterize Borders as: "The sweetest, gentlest dog in the home, fantastic with pups and people, but hard as nails in the field." All of their seven dogs are house dogs as well as workers.

Twelve years ago Ann Fargo of Larsen, Wisconsin, bought her first Border and started **Feorrawa**, after many years with Miniature Schnauzers. Miss Fargo is interested in obedience and trials, as well as conformation. She is active in the Great Lakes Border Terrier Club and an obedience instructor.

Terrier trials are the main interest of Cam and Bill Hall of Mt. Ulla, North Carolina. The adult **Swandell** Borders hold CGs and several of their dogs are champions. Their *Ch. Swandale's Sedgefield Scamp, CG* (Hunting Jack x Sedgefield's Whisper, bred by I. Milne) was best Working Terrier over several other breeds at one of the Virginia Hound Shows.

Joyce Kirn with dogs on daily two-mile walk, 1991.

Am. and Can. Ch. Behm Devlin, 1991. Photo by Tatham.

Von Hasselwick's Turtle Dove, Agility and Therapy Dog, with friend, 1991. Photo by Wichman.

Ruth Ann Naun with a group of Oldstone Borders, 1991.

Ch. Krispin Calirose Bentley, 1991.

Jan Hendricks, **Otterby Borders**, of Manhattan, Illinois, started with the foundation bitch *Ch. Saucy Debutante of But N Ben, CG* (Ch. Duttonlea Autocrat of Dandyhow ROM x Ch. Jollymuff Sweet Alyssum, bred by S. Howard and D. Jones) who died in late 1992. This kennel has produced several champions and most hold working titles. Mrs. Hendricks writes: "I particularly like the Borders because each one has a distinctive and different personality....I have fun with my dogs."

A very enthusiastic working and hunting Terrier owner is Barbara Kemp of **Steephollow Kennels**, Aiken, South Carolina. Mrs. Kemp has contributed the section on working Terriers for this book.

Wayne and Joyce Kirn of Bel Air, Maryland, give an interesting background for the kennel name, **Towzie Tyke**. It comes from Robert Burns' poem *Tam O'Shanter* in which Old Nick took the form of a *towzie tyke*, that is, a shaggy dog. Their first home-bred was *Towzie Tyke Nessie, CD, CG, WCh* (Ch. Major x Cotswold Dee Dee CD) who was a winner in trials, once with a five-second time! Among their several Borders is *Ch. Towzie Tyke Tweedle-Dee CD, CG, WCh*, who has had several group placements.

Robert and Arden LeBlanc of Galena, Ohio, were looking for a breed smaller than their Labrador Retrievers. In 1986, they found Borders to be the answer. Their first dog was *Ch. Todfield Tribute to Otterby* (Ch. Todfield Trafalgar Square Gold ROM x Ch. Saucy Debutante of But 'N Ben, bred by J. Hendricks). Since then, several winners have come from their **Hickory Ridge Kennel**, as well as more than 10 litters. "Borders are extremely adaptable," say the LeBlancs, who go on to write that they have been "extremely blessed with healthy, happy brown dogs who have not only made our lives richer, but also all the new owners."

Anita Moran, **Behm Borders**, of Ketchikan, Alaska, became interested in the breed in 1983: "Living in Alaska on the rocky, rainy coast, I wanted a small durable house dog that would be able to go with us in the boat but not be a fragile hot-house type companion." So her first dog was *Ch. Jocasta Just Hollywood, CG*, co-owned with Debra Blake (Ch. Springell Woodsmoke x Ch. Jocasta Just Sara, bred by L. Tofflemire and

D. Blake). Several champions have come from this kennel. Mrs. Moran is the columnist for the Canadian Kennel Club's official magazine and writes for several other publications.

Lawrenceville, Georgia, is the home of **Calirose Borders** owned by Vicky and Jim Sabo. They chose Borders as their second breed in 1986, and presently have three adults, all champions. Their *Ch. Krispin Calirose Bentley* (Ch. Woodlawns Dusky Gentleman x Ch. Steephollow Little Nell, bred by D. Corl and B. Kemp) was Best of Breed at the 1991 National Specialty Show. The Sabos are now starting in obedience work.

John and Laurale Stern live in Manitowoc, Wisconsin, and their kennel name is **Luvemur**. Starting in 1981, their kennel has expanded rapidly, and, in addition to conformation titles, the Sterns are adding obedience wins. In addition to nine bench champions, Luvemur dogs hold three CDs, three CDXs and one UD. Dr. and Mrs. Stern helped to found the very active Great Lakes Border Terrier Club.

Jane and Steven Worstell acquired their first Border in 1982 as a 4-H project for their daughter. By 1984, *Saga Hills Blue Jeans* was not only a holder of CDX but also TD and CG. Since then, the Worstells' **Tyneside Kennel** of Belton, Missouri, have added six Borders, and among them they have three bench champions, four CDs, three CDXs, one UD, three TDs and four CGs. In 1991, the Worstells' import *Ch. Hollybridge Raffles* (Eng. Ch. Dandyhow April Fool x Dandyhow Sweet Corn, bred by S.Williams) became the second UDT Border — the first was Ch. Chief of Lothian UDT, CG owned and trained by Nancy Hughes. "Rugby," as he's called, also has a CG.

Ch. Bever Lea Bewitching Brew, CD, 1991. Photo by Ashbey.

Ch. Royal Oaks Hurricane Hannah, CG, 1991. Photo by Bruni.

PART II
Breeding and Genetics

- *The Stud Dog*

- *The Bitch*

- *Genetics*

- *Newborn Puppies*

- *How to Read a Pedigree*

CHAPTER **5**

The Stud Dog

The dog you select to stand at stud should have certain things going for him. First, he should be masculine in appearance and, at least in your appraisal, conform closely to the breed Standard. A major mistake made by breeders is keeping a dog that is overdone in some features in the hope he can overcome a bitch with deficiencies in these areas. It doesn't work that way. It is futile to breed an oversize dog to a small bitch in the hopes of getting average-sized puppies. The hallmark of a good breeder, one who understands basic genetics, is breeding to dogs who conform to the Standard. Extremes should be avoided because they only add complications to a breeding program down the road.

Second, it is important that the stud dog come from a line of Border Terriers that has consistently produced champions on both his sire's and dam's sides. Such a line helps to ensure that he is likely to be dominant for his good traits. A bitch should also come from a good producing line. When a dog is found that has excellent producing lines for three generations on his sire's and dam's sides, there is an excellent chance that he will be a prepotent stud.

The third consideration is appearance. If the male is not constructed right, he is not going to be a great show dog. While the dog doesn't have to be a great show winner to attract the bitches, it helps. There are outstanding examples of non-titled dogs being excellent studs. However, they are somewhat rare.

There is more to breeding than just dropping a bitch in season into the stud dog's pen and hoping for the best.

A subject seldom discussed in the literature about stud dogs is the psyche of the dog. A young stud dog needs to be brought along slowly. If he is a show dog, he most likely has a steady temperament and is outgoing.

Early on, he should be taught to get along with other male dogs, but he should never be allowed to become intimidated. Good stud dogs have to be aggressive for breeding. Dogs who have been intimidated early seldom shape up. However, running, playing and even puppy-fighting with litter mates or other puppies don't have detrimental effects.

Until he is old enough to stand up for himself, the young male should be quartered first with puppies his own age and then introduced to bitches as kennel mates. It's not a good idea to keep him in a pen by himself. Socialization is extremely important. Time for play as a puppy and a companion to keep him from boredom helps his growth and development.

His quarters and food should present no special problems. Serious breeders all feed their dogs a nourishing and balanced diet. Studies in colleges of veterinary medicine and by nutritionists at major dog-food companies have shown that the major brands of dry dog food come as close to meeting the total needs of the dog as any elaborately concocted breeder's formula. Many breeders spice up the basic diet with their own version of goodies, including table scraps, to break up the monotony or to stimulate a finicky eater. However, this is more cosmetic than nutritional and is unnecessary. Dogs are creatures of habit and finicky eaters are man-made. Border Terriers are uniformly good eaters and doers. Do *not* get him fat and out of condition.

The most important aspect of being the owner of a stud dog is to make sure he can produce puppies. Therefore, at around 11 to 12 months of age it's a good idea to have a check on his sperm count by a vet. This will indicate if he is producing enough viable sperm cells to fertilize eggs. Sometimes it is found that while a stud produces spermatozoa, they are not active. The chances of this dog being able to fertilize an egg are markedly reduced. While this problem is usually found in older dogs, it does happen in young animals. Thus, the sperm count examination is important, and should be done yearly.

One should also be concerned with a stud dog's general health. Sexual contact with a variety of bitches may expose the dog to a wide range of minor infections and some major ones. Some, if not promptly identified and treated, can lead to sterility. Other nonsexual infections and illnesses, such as urinary infections, stones, etc., can also reduce a dog's ability to sire puppies. Since it is not desirable for any of these things to happen, stud dog owners need to be observant.

It's a good idea to have your vet check all incoming bitches. A stud-dog owner, however, should insist that the visiting bitch come with a veterinarian's certificate that the bitch is negative for canine brucellosis. While checking for obvious signs of infection, the vet can also run a smear to see when the bitch is ready to breed. The dog should also be checked frequently to see if there is any type of discharge from his penis. A dog at regular stud should not have a discharge. Usually he will lick himself frequently to keep the area clean. After breeding, it is also a good idea to rinse off the area with a clean saline solution. Your vet may also advise flushing out the penile area after breeding, using a special solution.

The testicles and penis are the male organs of reproduction. Testicles are housed in a sac called the scrotum. The American Kennel Club will not allow dogs who are bilateral cryptorchids (neither testicle descended) nor unilateral cryptorchids — monorchids — (dogs that have only one testicle descended) to be shown.

The male's testicles are outside the body because the internal heat of the body curtails the production of sperm. There is a special muscle that keeps them close to the body for warmth in cold weather and relaxes and lets them down to get air cooled in hot weather.

In the male fetus, the gonads, or sex organs, develop in the abdominal cavity migrating during gestation toward their eventual position. Shortly before birth they hover over an opening in the muscular structure of the pubic area through which they will descend to reach the scrotal sac. This external position is vital to the fertility of the animal, for production of live sperm can only proceed at a temperature several degrees cooler than normal body temperature. The glandular tissue of the testes is nourished and supported by arteries, veins, nerves, connective tissue and ductwork, collectively known as the spermatic cord. The scrotum acts as a thermostat.

As noted above, there are many involuntary muscle fibers that are stimulated to contract with the environmental temperature, pulling the testes closer to the body for warmth. Contraction also occurs as a result of any stimulus that might be interpreted by the dog as a threat of physical harm, such as the sight of a strange dog or being picked up. This contraction does not force the testicles back up into the abdominal cavity of the adult dog because the inguinal rings have tightened and will not allow them to be drawn back up. The tightening of the rings usually occurs at about 10 months of age.

There are a number of reasons why a dog may be a monorchid or cryptorchid. For example, the size of the opening through the muscles may be too small to allow for easy passage of the testes, or the spermatic cord may not be long enough for the testes to remain in the scrotum most of the time; and, as the proportions of the inguinal ring and testes change in the growing puppy, the time comes when the testes may be trapped above the ring as they grow at different rates. Also, there exists a fibrous muscular band that attaches both to the testes and scrotal wall, gradually shortening and actually guiding the testes in their descent. Possibly this structure could be at fault. The important thing about all of this is to help the prospective stud dog owner learn about the anatomy of the reproductive organs of the dog.

One should be gentle when feeling for a pup's testicles. The scrotal muscles may contract and the still generous inguinal rings may allow the disappearance of the parts sought.

It's a good idea to get the young stud dog started right with a cooperative, experienced bitch — one of your own preferably. By introducing the young and inexperienced stud to an experienced bitch, his first experience should result in an easy and successful breeding. A feisty, difficult bitch could very well frustrate the youngster, and as a result he may not be too enthusiastic about future breedings. Remember, one wants a confident and aggressive stud dog. There may be difficult bitches when he is an experienced stud, so it's best to bring him along slowly and gently for his first matings.

When the bitch is ready to breed (as your stud gains experience he will not pay too much attention to her until she is really ready) both animals should be allowed to exercise and relieve themselves just before being brought together. It's also a good idea not to feed them before mating. Bring the bitch in first. The place should be quiet and away from noise and other dogs. Spend a few minutes petting and reassuring her. Then bring the dog in on a lead. Do not allow him to come lunging in and make a frustrated leap at her. This can cause her to panic and bite him out of fear.

After a few minutes of pirouetting around together, she throwing her vulva in his face and him trying to lick fore and aft, take off the lead. Allow them to court for a few minutes. She should tell you she is ready by being coquettish and continually backing up into the dog.

Now comes the important time for the future success of the young stud: The dog needs to learn that the owner is there to help and should not back away from breeding the bitch just because someone is holding her.

Plan ahead and make sure there will be a large, nonskid rug on the floor. Place the bitch on the rug and face her rump toward the dog. Pat her on the fanny to encourage the dog to come ahead. Generally speaking, he will. As a rule he will lick her again around the vulva. Some dogs will go to the bitch's head and gently lick her eyes and ears. Encourage him, however, to come to the bitch's rear. If he is unsure of himself, lift the bitch's rear and dangle it in front of his nose.

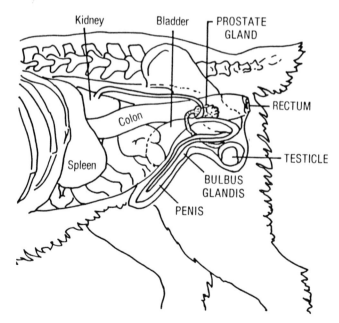

Figure 1. Stud dog.

Encouraged and emboldened, the male will mount the bitch from the rear and begin to probe slowly for the opening to the vulva. Once he discovers it, he will begin to move more rapidly. This is a critical time. Some young dogs are so far off the target they never get near the right opening. If this happens, gently reposition the bitch so he can have a better angle. This may occur any number of times. He may get frustrated and back off. Don't get excited as this is normal in a young dog. He may even get so excited and confused that he swings around and tries to breed her from the front.

Get him back on track. Again, gently get him to move to the bitch's rear and encourage him to proceed. At this time there may be a red, bone-like protuberance sticking out from the penis sheath. This, of course, is the penis itself. When, as a dog continues to probe and finds the opening, he will begin to move frenetically. As he moves in this fashion, a section just behind the pointed penis bone begins to swell. It is capable of great enlargement. This enlargement of the bulbous takes place due to its filling with blood, and it becomes some three times larger than the rest of the penis. In this way the dog, once having penetrated, is tied to the bitch; it is entirely due to the male, the bitch having no part in the initial tying.

When a tie has occurred, the semen is pumped in spurts into the vagina. The bitch then helps to keep the penis enlarged as she begins to have a series of peristaltic waves that cause a slight tightening and relaxing of the vagina. Some males will stay tied for up to one hour and others for as little as five minutes. A five-minute successful tie is just as satisfactory as a longer one because the semen has moved up through the uterus and fallopian tubes to the ovarian capsules by the end of five minutes.

Once the dog and bitch are successfully tied, the male may characteristically try to lift his rear leg over the bitch and keep the tie in a back-to-back position. Other dogs merely slide off the back of a bitch and maintain a tie facing in the same direction. It is always a good idea to have two people involved during the breeding, with one person at the bitch's head and the other at the male's.

Occasionally, a fractious bitch may be sent for breeding. She can be frightened about being shipped or spooked by strange surroundings. Certainly one doesn't want the dog to be bitten by a frightened bitch nor to have one's fingers lacerated. The easiest solution to this problem is to tie her jaws loosely with wide gauze. This muzzle should tie behind her ears to make sure it doesn't slide off. Pet her, reassure her, but hold her firmly during the breeding so she doesn't lunge at the dog.

After the tie has been broken, there sometimes will be a rush of fluid from the bitch. Don't worry about it, however, as the sperm is well up the fallopian tubes. Place the bitch gently in a quiet pen, apart from other dogs, and give her fresh water and an opportunity to relieve herself. The dog should be petted and praised. Once the dog is fully relaxed, be sure the penis is beck in the sheath. Then, he too should be put in a separate, quiet pen with fresh water. It's not a good idea to put him back with a group of male dogs.

How often can the dog be used at stud? If the dog is in good condition he should be able to be used every day for a week. Some serious breeders who, when faced with many bitches to be bred to a popular stud, have used the dog in the morning and the evening for at least three days. If a dog is used regularly, he can be used from day to day for a long time. However, if a dog is seldom used, one cannot expect him to be able to service bitches day after day for any great length of time.

Nature is most generous with sperm. In one good mating a dog may discharge millions, and a copious amount of sperm is produced in dogs who are used regularly. Frequent matings may be possible for a short time, but for good health and good management they should be limited to about three times a week. An individual bitch should be serviced twice — once every other day — for the best chance of conception.

For some breeders, breeding to a stud of their choice is often difficult, especially in countries that have quarantine restrictions. In the United States, the basic cost of shipping and the possibility of the dog being booked, the chance of making connections with a popular stud who is on a circuit being campaigned can produce a great deal of frustration. The use of frozen sperm opens up many new possibilities. At the time of this writing, there are 29 AKC- sanctioned collection stations. There should be many more in the near future.

Collecting sperm from dogs is not like collecting from cattle. One collection from the latter produces enough to inseminate more than 100 cows. The largest amount collected at one time over the many years of research in dogs was 22 vials. Usually two to three vials are used to breed a bitch two to three times.

The estimated time to store enough semen to inseminate 30 bitches differs by age, health, and sperm quantity and quality. Estimate approximately a month for a young dog, approximately three months for a dog of eight or nine years of age or older.

It doesn't take one long to recognize that, in the early stages, those males of outstanding quality will make up the main reservoir of the sperm bank. The collection centers suggest that collection be done at a young age, three to five years.

Limitations in quality and quantity due to old age lengthen the period necessary to store enough sperm for even a few bitches. In addition, the daily routine of a dog's life may limit freezability: The settling down in a new environment, changes in diet, water, or minor health problems. It is also not uncommon to get poor freeze results from a stud dog who has not been used for a month or longer. For the dog, once he settles down, the process of collection is a pleasant experience.

The following information on artificial insemination written by Diann Sullivan is reprinted by permission of *The Labrador Quarterly* (Hoflin Publishing Ltd., 4401 Zephyr St., Wheat Ridge, CO 80033-3299):

> Artificial insemination [AI] has been recognized as possible in dogs for some two hundred years. Semen is collected from the male and introduced into the reproductive tract of the female. When done properly, it is as successful as natural mating. It will not spoil a dog or bitch for future natural breedings and in fact, may desensitize a bitch to accept penetration.
>
> The main reason for AI failure is that it is used all too often as a last resort after trying and failing at natural breedings, when it is too late in a bitch's cycle for her to conceive. The use of artificial insemination as a back-up to a natural mating where a tie was not produced helps assure that as complete a mating occurred as was possible. Bitches who have had a vaginal prolapse and may

have scar tissue present after the protruding vaginal wall has been clipped and healed, may reject intercourse due to pain. It is also very useful when the stud dog manager finds he has a spoiled bitch in or one who has had little association with other dogs. Using an AI when natural mating is somehow impossible will provide a satisfactory service versus frustration on everyone's part.

The equipment needed includes one pair of sterile gloves (available through a pharmacy or your doctor), one inseminating rod (through dairy stores or International Canine Genetics), one 12 cc or 20 cc syringe (from stores, pharmacies), one artificial vagina and collection tube (ICG) or the sterile container that housed the syringe, a small piece of rubber tubing to attach the rod to the syringe and a non-spermicidal jelly (K-Y). To sterilize equipment after use, wash thoroughly in warm water and a drop or two of mild liquid dish soap. Rinse well with distilled water and dry completely with a hair dryer to avoid residual minerals that act as a spermicide.

On a safe surface within reach, lay out the package of sterile gloves, not touching the left glove to contamination. Glove your right hand with the right glove. On the sterile paper that the gloves are wrapped in, dispense a little jelly. Attach the collection tube to the smallest end of the artificial vagina (AV). Be sure it is securely in place. Roll down two plus inches on the large end of the AV to make it somewhat shorter. Place the AV and attached tube next to your body. We have the stud dog waiting in a crate within reach until the bitch is securely muzzled and standing ready.

The stud dog handler sits comfortably on a stool facing the bitch's left side. I use my left hand to support her stifle and can hold her tail out of the way with the same hand. Using the right hand, the stud dog helper pats the top of the bitch and encourages the stud dog to "get her!" The thumb and forefinger of the right hand grasps the bottom of the vulva to open it for easy penetration of the dog's erect penis, as he is actively mounting. When he is fully penetrated, the right hand can then hold the bitch's hock to add to the support the left hand is giving to her left stifle.

The stud dog may dismount without a tie occurring. If he is fully erect and dripping seminal fluid, the pre-warmed AV is slipped over his penis and held in place with the left hand. The right thumb and forefinger grasp the penis above the bulbous enlargement and apply steady pressure as the penis is pulled down and back for duration of the collection. If a collection is preferred without allowing penetration, the dog is stimulated into erection as he is actively mounting the bitch. Grasping the penis back behind the developing bulbous will produce thrusting at which time the AV is slipped over the enlarging penis. If collection is being done without an AV, the penis is brought down and back and the syringe container tube is carefully held under and away from the tip of the penis. The pressure from the right hand around the bulbous will cause the ejaculation which is carefully caught in the casing. Watch the collection tube fill. When you see a significant third and clear portion on top of the settled, thickened sperm, withdraw the AV.

Put the stud dog away in a kennel or area with enough room for him to safely retract his penis and in a clean environment. The bitch handler should sit comfortably on his stool and left the bitch's rear up over his knee so her rear is tilted up significantly.

Attach the inseminating rod to the syringe securely. Cut the rods to make them easier to handle. Slip the smooth end of the rod into the collection tube and all the way to the bottom. VERY SLOWLY (so as not to rip off those little sperm tails), draw up the seminal fluid into the syringe. Draw up an extra few cc's of air.

Carefully place the syringe and rod back inside your shirt for warmth, and carefully glove the left hand and apply the pre-dispensed K-Y jelly to the left fingertips.

Palm up, carefully insert the left third (middle) finger in and up to where the cervix can be felt. Gently slip your third fingertip just through the cervix. Carefully glide the inseminating rod along the palm side of the third finger to where the smooth tip can be felt by the fingertip. SLOWLY, use the syringe to pass the seminal fluid into the bitch. If you notice leakage, gently pass the finger tip and rod tip in a little further and continue to inseminate. Leaving the third finger in place during insemination acts as the body of the penis to block fluid loss.

Remove your finger after two minutes and continue to massage the vulva every thirty seconds or so, maintaining the tilt of her rear end for at least ten minutes. The massage of the vulva causes her vaginal canal to contract and pull the fluid up.

Crate the bitch for at least one hour after the breeding.

If the dog's sperm count is good and the sperm has good motility, breed three to four days apart to allow for the complete rebuilding of the stud dog's sperm count.

We must each continue to learn new and improved techniques to facilitate healthy pregnancies and practice methods that improve conception rates. Utilizing simple artificial insemination as a back-up to unsuccessful natural matings or as a choice in difficult matings increases the number of successful litters. AI allows the stud dog manager a reliable choice to assist his mating strategy for each bitch. AI is extremely useful in achieving a breeding early in the estrus, near when she may be ovulating. Following with either a successful natural mating or another successful AI every three or four days throughout her standing heat, would help insure that active sperm is available to the ripening ovum.

It is wonderful to receive the phone calls reporting the arrival of a litter that would not exist without the use of artificial insemination. Its reliability is constantly reinforced, and plays a strong role in improving conception rates.

The authors, however, must stress that natural breedings are preferable to artificial insemination. While extenuating circumstances with some bitches may necessitate AI, both the libido in the stud dog and the receptiveness of the bitch are inherited traits. In all his aspects, the Border Terrier is a natural dog, including his reproduction abilities. Reputable breeders never want to see the day when artificial means for breeding are the norm rather that the exception — as has happened to too many other breeds.

CHAPTER 6

The Bitch and Her Puppies

It has been said that a really good bitch is worth her weight in gold. Really good doesn't necessarily mean she will win Westminster. However, she should be a typical representative of the breed from a top-producing bloodline. In the previous chapter on the stud dog, emphasis was placed on a line of champion ancestors. This holds true in bitches as well, although it is somewhat harder to obtain because of the limited number of puppies they produce when compared to the male.

A bitch should be in good health before she is bred. Take her to the veterinarian to have her examined. This includes checking for heartworm and other parasites and making sure she is not carrying a sexually transmitted disease like brucellosis, a cause of sterility and abortions. All this should be done several months before she is due in season.

If there are any problems, they can be remedied. It is also important that the bitch is parasite free. Check for this once again just before she is to be bred as parasites can be debilitating to the puppies.

Her diet should continue along normal lines with plenty of exercise as she should be lean and hard. A fat bitch spells trouble in the whelping box.

Once she has been bred there is nothing special to do for the first few weeks. Again, a good, well-balanced diet, fresh water and normal exercise are extremely important. Most of the good commercial dry foods provide this. Slightly increase her food intake after the third week and feed her twice a day to make digestion easier. After week seven has gone by, feed her at the same level but spread the meals over three feedings. Throughout her pregnancy, she should be getting regular exercise. In the last three weeks, walk her briskly on lead, but don't let her physically overextend herself.

The average whelping time is sixty-three days after conception. No two bitches are alike and whelping can occur from the 59th day to the 65th day.

There are a number of things that can be done to prepare for the arrival of the puppies. First, prepare a comfortable, quiet place for the bitch to whelp. Either make or buy a whelping box. This box should sit above the floor a minimum of two inches to be out of drafts. It should have enough room for the dam to lie just outside an area where the puppies will snuggle but allow her some respite from them when she needs it. It should have a lip to keep the puppies in. It should also have enough room for her to whelp the puppies without feeling crowded and should allow an assisting person room to help. The whelping area should have a generous supply of newspaper to allow the bitch in labor to dig as she tries to nest. The floor itself should be covered with a rough surface like indoor-outdoor carpeting to allow the puppies to gain traction while they are nursing. After a few weeks, cover the area with newspaper because the mother will probably no longer clean up after the puppies, and it can get messy.

There should be an outside heating source either under the flooring or just above to make sure the puppies don't get chilled. Newborn puppies are unable to generate enough body heat to insulate themselves. It's imperative to supply that warmth externally. Listen for crying because this indicates something is wrong and it's often lack of warmth. Puppies will pile on one another to help keep warm. After about 10 days an external heat source is not as important. If the puppies are scattered around the box and not heaped together, the heat is too high.

There are some other supplies that are needed. Since the puppies usually don't come all at once, a place is needed to keep the puppies that have arrived in sight of the mother but out of the way as she whelps the next one. Most people use a small cardboard box with high sides. Get a clean one from your supermarket. At the bottom of this box put a heating pad or a hot water bottle. Cover it with a rough towel. Make sure it doesn't get too warm. After the dam has cleaned each puppy by roughly licking it with her tongue and drying it off, she may wish to nurse it. Let her try, but most of the time mother nature is telling her to prepare for the next whelp. If the bitch starts to dig at the papers on the floor of the box, remove the puppy and place it in the cardboard box. You may wish to leave the box in the corner of the whelping box. However, if the bitch starts to whirl around while whelping, take the box out. Be sure the bitch can see it at all times.

Clean, sharp scissors, alcohol and string should also be present. The scissors, which along with the string should be sitting in the alcohol, are to cut the umbilical cord if necessary. Cut the umbilical cord at least two inches from the puppy. Later, when the puppy is in the cardboard box, tie off the cord with the string. Disposable towels, washcloths, cotton swabs, toenail clippers, garbage pail and pans for warm and cold water are among the other supplies you should have on hand.

There should also be on hand a small syringe with a rubber bulb on it. These can be found in most drug stores and are called *aspirators* and are like the kind you use for basting, only smaller. If you can't find the proper tool, use your basting syringe. The purpose of this device is to clear the puppies' nostrils and lungs of excess fluid. Some puppies are born sputtering because fluid has accumulated in their nostrils or lungs in their trip through the birth canal. Try to suck the fluid from the nostrils first. Listen for a wheezing sound as this means there is still fluid. The puppy will also cough or choke. If all the fluid is still not out and the puppy is still sputtering, take the next step. Wrap the pup in the rough washcloth and grasping it under the chest and hindquarters, raise it above head level and then swing it down between your legs to try to give centrifugal force a chance to expel the fluid. Be firm but gentle — never do this violently. Repeat two or three times. Hold the puppy face down during this maneuver. This should do the trick. The heat in the bottom of the cardboard box should dry out any excess fluid.

As the time of whelping approaches, the bitch will have been giving all sorts of signs. In the last 10 days, her shape begins to change as the puppies drop down. As whelping approaches, she will seem restless and be unable to settle down for any length of time. She acts as though she can't get comfortable. She will also want a great deal of attention. She may or may not show an interest in the whelping box. Some bitches go to it, sniff around and walk away, while others lie in it and occasionally dig it up. Take her temperature on a regular basis as she grows more restless — 101.5° F is normal for a dog. Just before whelping she can take a sudden drop to about 98°. Unless the temperature drops, it's pretty sure there will be no immediate action. Some bitches, however, never have a temperature drop, so one can't rely on this indication. Most bitches whelp at night. There are exceptions to the rule — but be prepared. It's a good idea for someone to stay close by the whelping box to keep an eye on the bitch.

The most important sign to look for after her temperature starts to drop is the breaking of the water sac. There will suddenly be a small pool of water around her. This is often referred to as the *water breaking*. This means that real action is close at hand, at least in a matter of hours.

If her temperature goes down, the first thing is to alert the vet that a whelping is imminent and to stand by if any problems arise.

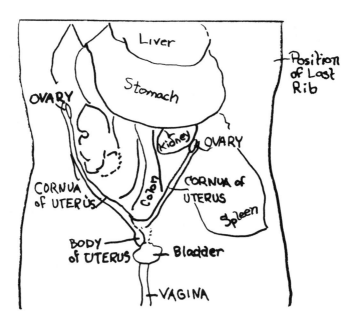

Figure 2. Bitch.

If this is the bitch's first litter, she may be a bit confused and frightened by all this. Reassure her often. Get her to the whelping box and make her comfortable. She may pace, she may dig or she may settle down, but allow things to proceed on their own. Let her go four or five hours if she seems in no distress. However, if she goes into labor and has not delivered a puppy, check with your vet. Labor means digging up papers, heavy panting, and straining followed by short rest periods. She may also issue large groans as she bears down. All this is normal if it is followed by the birth of a puppy.

As she bears down, sometimes standing in a defecating position, sometimes lying on her side, a sac will appear issuing from her vagina and with one big push, she will force it out. Usually, she will reach back and break the sac, cut the umbilical cord with her teeth, and start to lick the puppy to stimulate a cry. If she does not do so immediately or if she seems confused one must step in, cut the cord, and take the puppy out of the sac. One must then clear its lungs and nose and give it back to its dam to stimulate.

Many dams will eat the afterbirth, which is the bluish/black material attached to the sac the puppy came in. Let them eat a couple. It stimulates delivery of the next puppies. If she makes no move to do so, remove it and put it into a garbage pail. KEEP TRACK of the afterbirths. You need to make sure they are all accounted for. A retained afterbirth can cause great harm to the bitch. In fact, once she has finished whelping, be sure to take her to the vet to check her and make sure no afterbirths have been retained. The vet may give her a shot of pituitrin or similar drug to induce the uterus to contract and force out anything that's been retained.

Puppies may come one right after the other or there can be hours between deliveries. As long as she does not seem in distress, any pattern can be considered normal. If labor persists for a prolonged time and no puppies are forthcoming, call the vet even though she has whelped one or more puppies already. You may have a problem.

The vet will probably advise bringing her to the clinic where she can be examined to determine her problem. In most cases, it is usually only a sluggish uterus and the vet will give her a shot to speed things along and send her home to whelp the rest of the puppies. On occasion, there is a problem and he might opt to do a cesarean section by taking the rest of the puppies surgically. Usually, he will perform this surgery immediately. Some bitches have a problem and cannot even push the puppies down into the birth canal. The vet may take these puppies by "C" section without having her try to go into serious labor. It's a good idea to have another small box with a hot water bottle in it when you go to the vet so any puppies delivered there can be taken care of.

Now, whether the puppies have arrived normally or by C-section they are pursuing normal puppy behavior. Their primary concerns are keeping warm and being fed. A healthy dam will be able to take care of those needs. Be sure to keep a keen eye on both the dam and the puppies; watch for signs of distress. Crying, being unable to settle down, or looking bloated all mean trouble for the puppies. Call the vet. Watch the bitch to see if her discharge turns from a blackish color to bright red. See if she has milk and if the puppies can nurse from her. It is extremely important to stay vigilant for the next three weeks. It's a critical time.

It is helpful to understand how the size and sex of a litter are determined. One of the most informative and entertaining articles on the subject was written by Patricia Gail Burnham, a Greyhound breeder from Sacramento, California. Her article, "Breeding, Litter Size and Gender," appeared in an issue of the *American Cocker Review*. The following information is taken from this article. The number of puppies in a litter at whelping time is determined by several different factors. In the order in which they occur, they are:

1. The number of ova (gametes) produced by the dam
2. The number of ova that are successfully fertilized and implanted in the uterus
3. The prenatal mortality rate among the embryos while they are developing

It is not possible end up with more puppies than the number of ova that the bitch produces. As a bitch ages, the number of ova will often decrease. Bitches don't manufacture ova on demand the way a male dog can manufacture sperm. All the ova a bitch will ever have are stored in her ovaries.

In each season, some of them will be shed (ovulated) into her uterus for a chance at fertilization. Elderly bitches quite commonly produce two- or three-puppy litters. Sometimes, just living hard can have the same effect on a bitch as old age.

If a bitch does produce a large number of ova, what happens next? The ova need to be fertilized. If they are not fertilized, or if they are fertilized and not implanted, they will perish. If a bitch ovulates over an extended period of time and she is bred late in her season, the ova that were produced early may have died unfertilized before the sperm could reach them, and the result could be a small litter.

Sometimes there is a noticeable difference in birthweight. It is a good idea not to consider the small ones as runts. They may have been conceived a few days later than their larger litter mates and may grow up to be average-sized adults.

All the puppies in a litter are never conceived simultaneously, since all the ova are not released at once. Because ovulation takes place over an extended period, some of the puppies may be 59 days old while others may be 64 days old at birth. A few days' difference in puppies of this age can create noticeable differences in size.

The mature size of a dog is determined by its heredity and its nutrition. Its size at birth is determined by the size of its dam, the number of puppies in the litter, and its date of conception. The small puppies could just be more refined than the others and could always be smaller. Only time will tell.

The sire is always responsible for the sex of the offspring. The rule applies equally to people and dogs. While dams are often blamed for not producing males, they have nothing to do with the sex of their offspring. If the bitch determined the sex of the offspring, all the puppies would be bitches because the only chromosomes that a bitch can contribute to her offspring are those that every female has — homozygous (XX) sex chromosomes.

What's the difference between boys and girls? It's the makeup of their sex chromosomes. All of the chromosome pairs are matched to each other with the exception of one pair. Dogs (and people) have one pair of chromosomes that may or may not match. This is the chromosome pair that determines sex. Sex chromosomes may be either X chromosomes (which are named for their shape) or X chromosomes that are missing one leg, which makes them Y chromosomes (again named for their shape).

All females have two homozygous X chromosomes. They are XX genetically. All males are heterozygous (unmatched). They have one X and one Y chromosome to be XY genetically.

In each breeding, all ova contain an X chromosome, which is all a female can donate, while the sperm can contain either an X or a Y chromosome. If the X-carrying ovum is fertilized by an X-carrying sperm, then the result is female (XX.) If the X-carrying ovum is fertilized by a Y-carrying sperm, then the result is a male (XY).

What influences whether an X- or a Y-carrying sperm reaches the ovum to fertilize it? The Y chromosome is smaller and lighter weight than the X chromosome. This enables the Y-chromosome-carrying (male) sperm to swim faster than the heavier X-carrying (female) sperm. This gives the males an edge in the upstream sprint to reach the ovum that is waiting to be fertilized.

As a result, slightly more than 50 percent of the fertilized ova are male. More males are conceived than females. However, things even up, because males have a higher mortality rate than females, both in the womb and later.

What if ova are not ready and waiting when the sperm arrive? If sperm have to wait in the uterus or fallopian tubes for an ovum to arrive, then the odds change. Female sperm live longer than male ones. As the wait increases, the males die off and leave the female sperm waiting when the ovum arrives.

This is the reason that some breeders advise breeding as early as the bitch will stand to maximize the chance for female puppies. The idea is to breed, if she will allow it, before the bitch ovulates. This allows the male sperm time to die off and leaves the female sperm waiting when the ova arrive. Whether this has a basis in fact is not known.

What can influence the number of males and females in a litter other than the time of the breeding? The age of the sire can influence the gender of the puppies. As a stud dog ages, all his sperm slow down. Instead of a sprint, the race to fertilize the ova becomes an endurance race in which the female sperm's greater life span and hardiness can offset the male sperm's early speed advantage. When they are both slowed down, then the male sperm's higher mortality rate gives the female sperm the advantage.

CHAPTER 7

Genetics of the Border Terrier

BY MARGARET B. POUGH

The breeding of dogs is an art as well as a science. A successful breeder is one who consistently produces dogs of quality and shows overall breed improvement over the years. Successful breeders have an eye for a dog; they have learned to recognize quality when they see it. They also have some understanding of genetics, even if it is not defined. Progenies are the true test of any breeding program.

The many different breeds of dogs were developed through the process of mass selection — breeders chose dogs that had certain traits, and bred those individuals together. Desired traits were behavioral (good retrievers, hunters, sheep herders), physical, or both. Over the years, distinct types of dogs with specialized desirable behaviors and physical characteristics were developed. Dog breeds became recognized entities.

Purebred dogs are moderately inbred genetic isolates. Each breed has a higher probability of being homozygous at any gene locus than any mixed breed (Patterson & Pyle 1971). Border Terriers are highly inbred compared to many breeds. The population of Borders is quite limited compared to that of Labrador Retrievers or Beagles. About 3,000 Border Terriers are registered worldwide each year. Ten-generation pedigrees reveal a high number of ancestors in common among Borders. There are different types and different bloodlines in Borders, but the amount of variation available in the gene pool probably is more limited than it is in more numerous breeds.

Breeders look at specific traits and hope they can alter them by careful breeding and selection. In general, most characteristics are the result of many genes acting together; therefore selection to improve or change a trait can be slow and frustrating. Selection is a powerful tool; different breeds were developed by selection, but it is a slow process. We use selection every time we decide which dog to breed to which bitch. The phenotype we see is an expression of the genes present in the individual. We must remember that we are breeding the total dog, not just its head, or shoulder layback. The traits we are selecting for are influenced by many genes, and we may unknowingly be selecting for deleterious traits as well. Genetic defects occur in every breed. Borders are relatively free of genetic defects — but defects do occur, so breeders must be aware of them.

Genetics is the study of genes, and genes provide the *blueprint* that structures every organism. *Genes* are the basic unit of inheritance. Each gene occurs in a specific locus (place) on the chromosome. Various forms of a gene that occur at one locus are called alleles; each allele produces a different effect. A gene may have only one form, or it may have two or more alleles. Multiple alleles are quite common.

Genotype refers to the actual genes present in the individual, or the genetic blueprint. *Phenotype* refers to the result, what is seen, or the structure, color, and temperament of the dog.

Chromosomes occur in pairs and dogs have 39 chromosome pairs. A dog receives one member of each chromosome pair from each parent. Each chromosome may carry thousands of genes. The chromosomes of a pair each carry the gene for the same characteristic, but they may carry different alleles of that gene. Genes on a chromosome are linked and they usually are inherited together.

A dog that carries identical alleles on both members of a chromosome pair is homozygous for that pair of alleles (BB or bb genotype); a dog with different alleles is heterozygous (Bb genotype). The alleles of a gene usually can be arranged in the order in which they cover or mask the other alleles of that gene — a dominance series. An allele that completely masks the presence of another allele is said to be dominant. For example, the gene B produces black pigment and is completely dominant over its allele b that produces brown (liver) pigment; b is recessive to B. A recessive allele must be homozygous in order for its recessive phenotype to be expressed; i.e., a liver dog must be homozygous bb. Alleles that do not completely mask the presence of other alleles are incompletely dominant; they

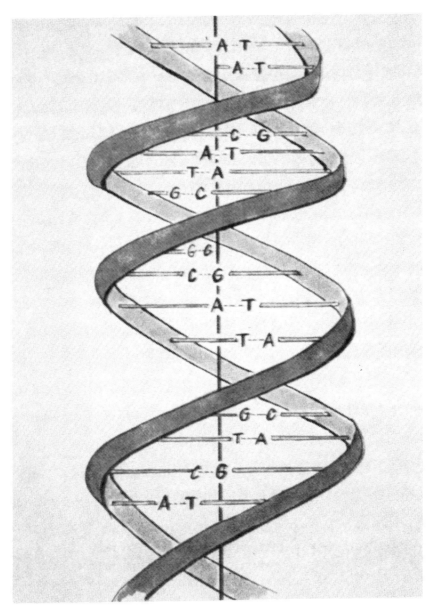

Figure 3. DNA structure.

produce an intermediate or mixed phenotype in the heterozygote. A dominant allele with incomplete penetrance is one in which the dominant phenotype is expressed in the heterozygote only when certain conditions are met, such as other genes being present or specific environmental requirements.

The phenotype, what is actually seen, is a result of genes that have acted throughout the development of the dog. The genes act *in utero*, in the whelping box, and as the dog grows and matures. The physical surroundings, nutrition, the health of the dam and growing puppy, and the psychological setting in which the dog is raised can influence the expression of genes. Some genes have profound effects by themselves. Most genes act in concert with many other genes and the results can be influenced by the milieu in which they occur. Behavioral traits have a genetic basis just as do physical traits. The ability of a Border Terrier to *sing* has a strong genetic component. All the pups sired by one dog could sing very well, and it varied in his grandchildren. Dogs can learn to sing, but the true singers stand out — they sing early and melodiously. The genes form the blueprint, or basis, of the organism. Just as two houses with the same blueprints can look entirely different when completed, two dogs with the same basic genes can look and act differently. The entire dog — size, color, conformation, temperament, and behavior — has a genetic blueprint.

Coat color is a polygenic system (dependent on many genes acting together) for which many of the genes have been described. There are at least nine genes that affect coat color in dogs. Some color genes have only two alleles while others may have four or five different alleles. Some breeds are heterozygous at many loci; the breed has a wide range of colors. Other breeds are homozygous for most color alleles; the breed has only one or two colors. All dogs have one gene present for each characteristic, even if the gene is represented by only one allele. Because the influence of the environment is limited, a look at coat color may help explain the complexities of a polygenic system.

ALLELES OF COLOR GENES POSSIBLY PRESENT IN BORDER TERRIERS								
Agouti	Melanin Color	Color Depth	Recessive Dilution	Extension	Dominant Graying	Merle	Spotting	Ticking
aY	B	C	D	Em	G		S	
at	b	cch	d	E	g	m		t

Most of the color variations in Borders are the result of interactions between the alleles at the Agouti and Extension loci. Borders have at least two alleles of the agouti (A) gene; sable (aY) produces the red-tan color, and tan points (a^t) is recessive and produces blue and tan when homozygous (a^{t}a^t). At the extension (E) locus there are also two alleles: super-extension (E^m) causes a black mask on muzzle and ears, normal extension (E) allows dark pigment to develop where allowed by the A alleles. Both the A and E gene alleles present in Borders exhibit incomplete dominance. Clear red dogs are probably homozygous for both sable and normal extension (aYaYEE). Dogs that are heterozygous for either blue and tan (aYa^t) or super-extension (E^{m}E) will show a greater amount of grizzling, as well as darker muzzle and ears. Individuals homozygous for super-extension will have dark muzzles, ears and dark grizzle heads. The amount of grizzling on the body may increase as well. Since the amount of grizzling can vary from the very dark silver-grizzles to those with only a few dark hairs interspersed in the sable, there are probably other modifying genes. Dark silver-grizzles can be distinguished from blue and tan by the color of the undercoat. Blue and tans always have blue-black undercoat where the topcoat is blue.

The color depth (C) locus determines the richness of the phaeomelanin (red-tan) pigment. The alleles present in Borders exhibit incomplete dominance. Homozygous CC dogs are a deep, foxy-red, while homozygous ^{Cch}C$_{ch}$ dogs are pale tan. Heterozygous individuals are intermediate in color. Again, other modifying genes may be present that increase the range of red-tan color that is seen.

The recessive alleles at the B and D loci are found in Borders. The B locus determines the color of the melanin pigment. Most

Borders have black pigment (BB), but the recessive allele for liver (bb) has been recorded. Recessive dilution (dd) produces pups that are bluish gray with a slate nose (or pale brown if bb dd). The gene frequency for b and d is low and true liver or dilute Borders are very rare. It appears that the alleles had a higher gene frequency in the past. British breeders report greater color variation in the past. (Roslin-Williams 1976, Orme 1972, Gardner 1985)

Dominant graying (G) has been postulated as occurring in Borders (Willis 1989). The progressive graying seen in blue and tans does not appear to be the same as seen in breeds known to carry G (Old English Sheepdogs, Kerry Blues). Borders are probably normal (gg).

Borders are non-merle (mm), non-spotted (SS), and probably non-ticked (tt). White chest and toe spots are not alleles of the spotting gene. Modifying genes explain the color variants that are not covered by these defined color genes. For a review of coat color in Border Terriers see the *1971 Breed Book* (Pough 1972).

The Genetics and Research Committee of the Border Terrier Club of America has compiled a database of defects that occur in the breed. The committee collects information on litters and on dogs that have exhibited defects. Identity of dogs is kept confidential. The type of defect and what is known about its incidence in the breed, its incidence in dogs, its heredity, and suggestions for eliminating the problem from the breed, are published in the BTCA newsletter, *The Borderline*. When familial tendencies are noted in the occurrence of a defect, an inherited defect is suspected. When defects are rare, it is difficult to determine if there is a genetic basis unless breeders cooperate through the Genetics Committee. Insults occurring during embryonic development of a litter may profoundly affect normal maturation and congenital defects may occur. Insults include physical trauma, exposure to toxic chemicals, and bacterial and viral infections. Radiation exposure may be both teratogenic and mutagenic. The database of the Genetics Committee can help determine whether a defect is inherited or a congenital accident.

Heart defects have been identified in Border Terriers (as in most breeds). Ventricular septal defects (VSD) are very rare, but a familial occurrence is known. The relatively limited gene pool means that all breeders should be aware of the problem. All genetic heart defects in dogs appear to have a polygenic mode of inheritance (Patterson & Pyle 1971).

A group of Borders (all related) was studied at the University of Guelph, Ontario, in 1969-70. The dogs exhibited premature degeneration of the heart muscle. The problem has not been reported since then. Patent ductus arteriosus has been reported in a few Borders and as some of these are related, the defect may be inherited. Other heart defects identified in Border Terriers include tetralogy of Fallot (TOF), pulmonary stenosis, and atrial septal defect. The incidence of these defects is low. Most Borders with heart defects live relatively normal lives, even those with TOF and VSD. However, no Border with a defect should be used for breeding. Borders that have siblings with VSD or those that have produced VSD have a much higher chance of passing on defective genes than others. All Border Terrier puppies should be checked for heart murmurs before leaving the breeder. Borders with murmurs should be referred to a veterinary cardiologist so that a diagnosis can be made.

Canine hip dysplasia (CHD) occurs in Borders. Hip dysplasia has a polygenic mode of inheritance with a high environmental influence on its development — excessive nutrition, fast growth rates, and poor footing have all been implicated in the expression of the defect. All breeding stock should be determined to be clear by means of radiographs. X-rays should be interpreted by the Orthopedic Foundation for Animals (OFA) or a board certified radiologist.

Progressive retinal atrophy (PRA) is known in Borders. When PRA is diagnosed late, an individual could have been bred many times, as could its parents. Other eye abnormalities that appear to be inherited in Borders include: juvenile subcapsular cataracts (appearing before age seven); multifocal retinal dysplasia (retinal folds); and a fundus variation that mutes the reflectance of the peripheral tapetum (Rubin 1989). PRA and cataracts influence the vision of the affected dog. All breeding stock should have yearly eye examinations by a board certified veterinary ophthalmologist. PRA is believed to be inherited as a simple recessive in most breeds. Any dog that has produced an affected individual is a carrier and should be removed from the breeding population. Breeders must be on the alert even though the gene frequency is very low. If every Border had an eye exam between the age of three and four years, the large body of data accumulated would contribute to the understanding of PRA and other eye defects in the breed.

Patellar and hock joint laxity and Leggs-Perthes syndrome (aseptic necrosis of the femoral head) have been reported. Joint laxity may be related to the overall conformation of the hind leg. Leggs-Perthes may be inherited in some breeds (Kirk 1986) but, in general, the cause is not simple (Nebzydoskl 1982, Ross 1986). Any insult that disturbs the normal maturation process of epiphyseal junction of the femoral head may cause the syndrome. Progressive degeneration is common in breeds in which the syndrome appears to have a genetic basis.

Tail abnormalities include kinked tails and abnormally short tails. The inheritance is probably polygenic. Many breeders consider these cosmetic defects. They are skeletal abnormalities, and all breeders should be aware of the incidence in their bloodlines. There is an increased incidence in the occurrence of kinked and screw tails reported to the Genetics Committee. Borders have a naturally, relatively short tail, but the very short *natural docks* should not be used for breeding. Tail length is polygenic and where selection favors the tailless individual, spinal abnormalities may occur (Burns & Fraser 1966).

Primary uterine inertia due to conscious inhibition of labor was reported in Border Terriers by Freak (1965). She found inertia in kennel dogs brought into the house to whelp, but also noted that pet bitches of many breeds exhibited inertia if isolated for whelping. Bitches should be acclimated to the whelping area well before their due date. Genetics Committee records do not indicate that primary inertia is a problem. Secondary inertia is the main cause of cesarean sections, usually because of large whelps or malpresentations.

Cryptorchidism is the failure of one or both testicles to descend into the scrotum. Clark and Stainer (1983) list a recessive inheritance for cryptorchidism in Border Terriers. Gardner (1985) concluded from breeding studies using a monorchid dog that a simple recessive mode of inheritance was not supported in Border Terriers. Some male Border Terriers have testicles that are slow to descend, yet mature with two normal testicles present in the scrotum. Other male pups have both testicles descended by eight weeks of age. The extremes can be found within one litter.

Familial clusters of Borders that have seizures have been reported. Seizures may have many causes: trauma, hypoglycemia, toxicity, and genetic defects. Some Borders with classical epilepsy have been reported, but these do not show a familial relationship. Seizures in the familial clusters vary in frequency and severity — some are mild while others are of the grand mal type. The incidence is low, but the familial pattern indicates a probable genetic basis.

Undershot bites occur in the breed. Adult occlusion can not be determined until after dentition replacement when the jaw proportions stabilize — usually by seven months of age. If the canines mesh properly the dog can still do its job, but level or undershot incisors may be prematurely lost. In determining occlusion the meshing of the incisors, canines, and premolars should be examined. The occlusion of the first premolar is a key marker. The first premolar of the lower jaw should be just in front of the first premolar of the upper jaw, and the following premolars should interdigitate. Some dogs have one incisor out of line; this often happens when the lower incisors erupt before the corresponding upper incisor. In these individuals, it is important to be sure the jaw is normal by examining premolar position on both sides. Wry jaws occur in Borders as in other breeds. Missing teeth, in the adult dentition, have been reported. The different elements of the head are not inherited as one unit; instead, the entire head structure depends on many genes. In all dentition defects the ultimate test is in the progeny. Selecting for good occlusion means removing from the breeding population those individuals that consistently produce malocclusion. Know the occlusion of the individuals you are breeding, and the occlusions of their sibs, parents and grandparents.

METHODS OF CONTROLLING GENETIC DEFECTS

The process of selection against genetic defects depends on the mode of inheritance, the severity of the defect, the incidence within a breed, and the importance of the defect to breeders. Defects that are caused by a dominant gene are the easiest to eliminate because every carrier can be identified and removed from the breeding population.

Simple recessives can be hidden for many generations, especially if the frequency of the gene is low. However, if a defect is known to be caused by a simple recessive gene, its incidence can be reduced if breeders are willing to remove all affected animals, including their parents and siblings, from the breeding population. When a defect is caused by a simple recessive, an affected pup means that BOTH parents are carriers and 50 percent of all their phenotypically normal offspring may be carriers (Hutt 1979). Test breeding may indicate if an individual is a carrier. Test breed a dog in question to an affected individual; if there are no affected pups, and at least six normal progeny, the probability is only 0.0156 (1 in 64) that the tested dog is a carrier. With seven normal progenies, the probability improves to 0.0078 (1 in 128). Test breeding stud dogs is particularly important, because most stud dogs have a greater number of offspring than do brood bitches. If laboratory tests can determine carriers, such tests should be used on all potential breeding stock, and carriers should be eliminated from breeding plans.

Test breedings can determine more complex inheritance, and can use a known carrier rather than an affected dog; such schemes, however, need to be carefully planned. Progenies need to be maintained and monitored, and it may take a number of generations before the inheritance can be determined. Few breeders have the time or space to maintain test breeding populations. Breeders can help geneticists by keeping careful records. Such records should include normal and abnormal pups in litters, pups that are born dead or died before weaning, and information on dogs as they mature. Breeders should be willing to communicate with other breeders and with the Genetics Committee. Sibling data are equally important to maintain as the data on affected dogs. Such data can enable geneticists to do analyses that may elucidate information on suspected genetic defects.

Most defects are polygenic; they are caused by many genes acting together. Polygenic defects are difficult to eliminate. Where possible, test for the defects with x-rays or blood tests. Remove affected individuals from the breeding population.

Rely on progeny tests to determine the suitability of individual sires and dams. If an individual produces a large number of affected offspring (even though clear itself), remove it from the breeding population.

These same principles apply to selecting to improve type.

Score the entire dog, and select overall outstanding individuals as breeding stock. Select for breeding those individuals that consistently produce the desired qualities. Hutt (1979) advises against inbreeding (mating of close relatives) and suggests linebreeding (matings based on a common ancestor, but not close relatives) in order to keep defects associated with homozygosity at a minimum.

Breeders linebreed to develop and maintain desired type. However, homozygosity increases for both desired and undesired characters. Linebreeding solely on the basis of a famous individual in a pedigree is mere name dropping. Any breeding program should be based on knowledge of past generations. Look at the progeny of the grandparents as well as the progeny of the dogs that are being considered for breeding. Look at weak points as well as strong points and do not be afraid to ask questions of the owners.

The low population of Borders contributes to homozygosity within the breed, yet the different types indicate that genetic diversity still exists. Diversity is important to maintain because it gives breeders the chance to select for normal genes when genetic defects appear. Borders have few genetic defects compared to many other breeds. The presence of a defect cannot be blamed on any one individual. Mutations can occur in any gene at any time. The extensive use of a normal sire that carries a defect can increase the gene frequency of the defective gene in the population. Testing for known defects, maintaining accurate records, and sharing information will help reduce or eliminate defects and identify new ones if they occur.

Border puppy, V. and J. Sabo, 1991.

CHAPTER 8

Problems of Newborn Puppies

Breeding and raising puppies is a complex process, and many factors determine the survival rate of the pups. The health of the dam, the absence of parasites, the cleanliness of the environment and the quality of care are the controlling factors that govern survival. Environment and hereditary, either before or after birth, determine whether puppies develop along normal lines.

NURSING

Bruce R. Wittels, D.V.M., writing in the January/February 1985 issue of the *Great Dane Reporter* states:

> The ability to nurse is the most important factor in determining whether a newborn pup will survive the first few hours and days of life. Nursing ability depends upon the maturity of the litter, body temperature and adequate lung function. If a bitch is underfed or improperly nourished before and during pregnancy, the likelihood of premature whelping is greatly increased. This leads to underdevelopment of the lungs and therefore failure of the lungs to fully oxygenate the blood. This limited respiratory capacity causes a decreased nursing time due to more time needed for breathing. With a premature whelping there is a lack of subcutaneous fat on the newborn and as a result a decreased body temperature and chilling. Because of this, energy is expended to keep the body as warm as possible and less energy is available for nursing. Diminished nursing ability is

directly caused by chilling as well as lack of energy secondary to it. Therefore, it is important not to let the litter become chilled no matter what the cause.

It is very important that the pups suckle within the first few hours. The ingestion of nutrients gives them energy and strength since they are no longer being nourished by the placenta. Colostrum is only present in the mammary glands for four to six hours and nursing during this time provides maternal immunity to many viral and bacterial diseases. The puppy acquires some maternal immunity via the placenta during pregnancy, but the most important acquisition is by the ingestion of colostrum. If a pup isn't nursing, it must be placed on a nipple and encouraged to do so. It may be necessary to milk the bitch and force feed the pup. If all efforts are unsuccessful, put the pup on antibiotics, watch it closely, and keep it confined until it can be started on a series of adult vaccines.

Most people know that at six weeks of age their dogs need to be vaccinated, but apparently what isn't known is which vaccines are given. Almost all puppies seen in my practice that have been previously been vaccinated have been given an adult vaccine at six weeks of age; i.e., Distemper, Hepatitis, Leptospiroses, and Parvovirus combination — this is not proper. If the bitch had previously been vaccinated, this vaccine has no beneficial effect and can do possible harm.

Colostrum contains many antibodies called immunoglobulins which function to destroy bacteria and viral infections to which a pup is exposed. These immunoglobins last for approximately eight to ten weeks. If an adult vaccine is used at six weeks of age they act as foreign viruses and are destroyed by the antibodies of maternal immunity. This vaccine can be injurious to the animal if it is simultaneously being infected with the real disease entity. The specific immunoglobulins are then divided between destroying the real infection and the vaccine. If the viral strength is more than that of the antibodies, the body will succumb to the disease.

Many immunologists believe that six week old dogs should be vaccinated with a human measles vaccine and a killed parvo virus vaccine. Human measles vaccine boosts the maternal immunity against canine distemper and does not challenge it. A killed parvovirus vaccine is used due to the lack of transmission of adequate antibodies from the bitch to properly protect the pups for more than six weeks. This vaccination will often help to stimulate the pups own immune system to produce antibodies against this potentially deadly virus.

Otterby puppies, 1988. L-R: Ch. Saucy Debutante of But'N Ben, CG, Ch. Otterby A Klever Kelsey, CG, Rycar Otterby Bluer Than Blue, Ch. Otterby's Catcher in the Rye, CG, Otterby Right on Target, CG.

Puppies should nurse for three to four weeks. During this nursing period the major emphasis is on nutrition of the mother, as all of the dietary needs of the litter are derived from her. With a very large litter, or if the dam is not producing enough milk, the diet should be supplemented with such milk replacements as *Esbilac* or *Unilac*. A pup should be gaining weight daily at the rate of approximately one gram for each pound of body weight expected at maturity. However, attempts to over-supplement in order to reach this goal are highly inadvisable. The following table, abstracted from *Lab Report 2, #4 Neonatal Puppy Mortality*, was prepared by the Cornell Research Laboratories, Veterinary Virus Research Institute, New York.

WEIGHT GAIN
Two fold increase at 8-10 days
(1 gm of expected adult weight/day)

BODY TEMPERATURE
week 1-2; 94-99°F
week 2-4; 97-100°F

WATER REQUIREMENTS
2-3 oz/lb/day (newborn puppies)

CALORIC REQUIREMENTS
60-100 kcal/lb/day (newborn puppies can become
hypoglycemic if not fed every day)

PARASITES

An unfavorable environment may seriously hinder normal development before birth as well as afterward. The prenatal environment provided for the growing embryo may be unsuitable because the mother has been improperly fed and cared for during pregnancy or because she is infested with worms. Even though nature will rob the mother to feed the unformed young, the puppies may be so lacking in vitality as the result of malnutrition that they are either born dead or die shortly after birth. Newborn puppies suffering from malnutrition are not necessarily skinny puppies. They may be well formed and appear to be healthy, but, like adult dogs that have become fat on an unbalanced diet and lack of exercise, they may be anemic and so weak they are unable to cope with the difficulties encountered during birth and unable to adjust themselves successfully to the new environment. Puppies born with worms acquired from their dam may not show signs of illness until they are three or four weeks of age when they may sicken and die very quickly. There are a number of worm infestations that a breeder needs to be concerned about. People have misconceptions about internal parasites. Some think dogs can be immunized against them. Others apparently think that when parasites are removed that is the end of them. Others have the idea that when a dog is a year old he is no longer susceptible to them. There is no time in a dog's life when he is immune to parasites, but in certain cases, such as coccidiosis, he is more likely to be infected when he is quite young. Because information concerning the proper care of the bitch during pregnancy and the prevention of worm infestations is readily available today, malnutrition and parasites need not be major causes of puppy losses.

INJURIES

Injuries received either before or after birth may result in the death of one or more puppies in a litter — in spite of the fact that every precaution may have been taken to prevent such injuries. In the case of a large litter, but even in a small- or average-size litter, the embryos may be crowded together too closely to allow for proper development, which may result in distortions or the premature birth of small, weak puppies.

Carelessness on the part of a nervous or inexperienced bitch undoubtedly accounts for the loss of many puppies that are born alive and appear to be strong and healthy at birth. Even the best of mothers may occasionally sit or lie on a puppy, crushing or smothering it.

The bitch's endocrine system, which is responsible for the secretions of such important glands as the thyroid, pituitary, adrenals and reproductive glands, may fail to work properly during pregnancy because of disease or hereditary factors, resulting in the arrested development or malformation of the embryos or in the premature birth of the litter. Abnormal functioning of the endocrine system may also cause various mating and whelping difficulties, such as dystocia (painful or delayed delivery) and lack of an adequate milk supply, which may account for puppy losses. If an inadequate amount of endocrine secretions (hormones) is produced within the unborn puppy itself, its development may be temporarily or permanently stopped at any stage. If development is arrested in the early stages, the partly formed embryo or embryos affected may be aborted or re-absorbed by the bitch, or they may remain dormant in a *petrified* state awaiting the termination of gestation. If development is arrested in latter stages, the embryo may be born alive but malformed.

Many so-called freaks are the result of arrested development during the embryonic stage, resulting in such malformations as a harelip, cleft palate, cleft abdomen or cleft skull. All of the malformations are the result of the parts of the embryo failing to unite properly during development. If this failure is complete, any part of the embryo may be disunited by a deep cleft that may affect one side of the body more than the other, or it may affect both sides equally. If the growth of the embryo is retarded in a very late stage of development, only a slight cleft or other malformation may mar its perfection.

An analysis of litter records done by the Roscoe B. Jackson Memorial Laboratory indicates a higher percentage of puppies are stillborn or die shortly before birth in the first litter than in the second, third, fourth and fifth litters. In a study of 337 litters, the percentage of dead puppies in the first litter was 5.7 percent, while in the fourth litter the percentage was 2.0 percent and in the fifth litter 2.8 percent. Because the cause of death could not be determined accurately in most cases, it is assumed that inexperience on the part of the bitch in whelping and caring for her first litter is partly responsible for the higher death rate. After the fifth litter, however, the death rate increased considerably, the percentage of dead puppies in the sixth litter averaging 18.7 percent. However, the steady decrease in incidence of death until the fourth or fifth litters indicates intra-uterine conditions in older bitches are more likely to be unfavorable for the production of normal young.

FADING PUPPIES

Fading puppy syndrome is often confused with toxic milk syndrome. It is estimated that 28 percent of all puppies die in the first week after birth. Some of these puppies suffer from lethal congenital defects, maternal neglect or accidents, such as being crushed in a whelping box. A large proportion of them, however, die from what is defined as the fading puppy syndrome. The syndrome is part of a specific disease entity but perhaps the true fading puppy is the individual who (1) was born malnourished because its dam did not receive adequate nutrition during gestation, (2) is too weak to nurse effectively, (3) is not receiving an adequate supply of milk, (4) is in an environment that is not sufficiently warm, or (5) a combination of these factors. Unless supplementary feeding is started within a few hours of birth, with frequent weight checks to monitor progress, and unless adequate heat is provided, these puppies become chilled, weak, and ultimately fade and die.

Newborn puppies differ physiologically from adult dogs in several important ways. It is necessary to understand these differences to realize why puppies succumb rapidly to stress and to appreciate the importance of proper environment and care. They have body temperatures of 94° to 97°F for the first two weeks of life as compared to the adult dog's normal temperature of 100° to 101.5°F. They do not have a shivering reflex until about six days of age and thus cannot maintain body heat. Their heart beats and respiratory rates are faster than the adult dog. Newborns must be kept in an environmental temperature of 85° to 90°F for the first week of life; the temperature is gradually decreased to 70°F by the time the puppies are weaning age. They should gain 1 to 1 1/2 grams daily for each pound of anticipated adult weight and should double birth rate in eight to ten days.

Border Terrier puppy, V. and J. Sabo, 1991.

NEONATAL SEPTICEMIA

Neonatal septicemia affects puppies from one to four days of age. It is caused by a staphylococcus infection in the vaginal tract of the bitch, transmitted to the puppy at birth. An unclean environment should not be overlooked as a precipitating factor in the disease.

Infected puppies have swollen abdomens with bluish discoloration on the flanks. They cry, are hypothermic, dehydrated and refuse to nurse. Death occurs 12 to 18 hours after bloating and crying unless antibiotic treatment is started immediately. Supportive therapy (heat, glucose and water), described under *Puppy Septicemia*, also must be administered.

Prevention involves a pre-breeding veterinary examination with antibiotic therapy if necessary to counteract infection. Since an unsanitary environment is frequently involved in neonatal (and puppy) septicemia, kenneling should be clean as well as everything else to which the newborn puppies are exposed. This includes your hands and the scissors used to cut the umbilical cords. The cords should be dipped in or swabbed with iodine.

PUPPY SEPTICEMIA

Puppy septicemia is the leading cause of death by disease in infant puppies, occurring from four to forty days of age. It happens typically in vigorous puppies that were born normally and are efficient nursers. Illness is sudden. First one puppy starts to cry. It has abdominal distention, diarrhea and may have rapid respiration. Then it refuses to nurse, becomes dehydrated and loses weight rapidly. Death usually follows 18 hours after onset of symptoms. Another puppy becomes sick, then another and another. Septicemia can demolish most or all of a litter within five to six days.

It is caused by bacteria of the streptococcus, staphylococcus, escherichia or pseudomonas types and frequently is associated with a metritis or mastitis (inflammation of the womb or of the breasts) infection in the bitch. Metritis is a uterine infection that may be acute or chronic. In the acute phase, the bitch becomes ill soon after the litter is whelped, depressed with an abnormal vaginal discharge, and a temperature that may rise to 104°F. Chronic metritis may not cause overt symptoms in the bitch and, in fact, may not be evidenced until she whelps stillborn puppies or puppies that succumb to infection shortly after birth. Mastitis is painful and fever producing for the bitch. It can transmit bacterial infection to the litter.

Sick puppies are chilled, have low blood sugar and are dehydrated. Immediate concerns are to counteract these conditions. Otherwise, the puppies will die too quickly for any therapy to be effective. They must be taken from the bitch and the following actions taken:

For chilling: slow warming. The sick puppy's body temperature has usually fallen to 78° to 94° F. It must be placed in an environmental temperature — incubator, heat lamp or heat pad — of 85° to 90°F until body temperature has risen to normal for the infant puppy. Circulation must be stimulated by frequently turning and massaging the puppy during the slow warming process. Only the surfaces of the puppy's body will be warmed if this is not done. Temperature of the newborn puppy can be taken with an infant's rectal thermometer. Hold the puppy up by the base of the tail and insert the thermometer one-half inch into the rectum. Environmental temperature can be monitored with an inside thermometer on the floor of the whelping box or incubator. Relative humidity should be 55 to 60 percent; this can be accomplished by using a home humidifier in the room in which the whelping box is placed.

For low blood sugar (hypoglycemia): glucose therapy. The sick puppy's blood sugar must be increased rapidly and the administration of glucose solution, which is absorbed directly into the stomach, is the best way of doing this. Give the puppy 5 to 15 percent glucose in water, orally, 1 to 2 c.c. (milliliters) every half hour. As the puppy's condition improves, gradually increase the dosage to 4 to 6 c.c. These puppies should not be given formula; it may not be absorbed and thus may cause intestinal blockage.

For dehydration: water, given orally. The glucose and water therapy described above should be sufficient. If the puppy's condition is extremely serious, the veterinarian may think it advisable to administer subcutaneous hydrating solutions.

Other therapy, recommended by the veterinarian, may be to give antibiotics in some cases. Gamma globulin serum is considered effective. The owner may also be asked to give the puppies commercial formula or a few drops of *very fresh* liver juice every few hours after they have started to rally; this is strength enhancing.

Prevention starts with a pre-breeding veterinary examination of the bitch. Bacterial culture and sensitivity testing should be performed on specimens removed from the vagina. These tests should be mandatory when a bitch has a history of uterine infection, stillborn puppies or puppies that die soon after birth from bacterial infection. Appropriate antibiotic therapy should take place before breeding if the bitch tests positive. It may be advisable to have another course of antibiotics 48 hours before whelping and immediately after whelping. In no case should this be done haphazardly; antibiotics should be given only when necessary and under veterinary supervision.

Every effort should be made to have all the puppies take colostrum. This protects the puppy from disease for the first weeks of its life. Lack of colostrom seems to be among the precipitating factors of puppy septicemia.

The bitch should be in a state of nutritional good health, fed ample quantities of a good-quality commercial dog food product recommended for gestation and lactation. A feeding alternative is a complete and balanced puppy food product. Its high caloric density and protein content are advantageous for the gestating or lactating bitch. Liver, one half ounce per thirty pounds, is considered an excellent food supplement for the gestating bitch, contributing to the strength and vigor of the newborn litter.

Kenneling should be clean and well ventilated with appropriate temperature and humidity. Unsanitary quarters will predispose the litter to disease.

CANINE HERPES VIRUS (PUPPY VIREMIA)

This is another leading cause of death in young puppies, transmitted at whelping as puppies pass through the vagina of a recently infected bitch. Puppies can also be infected by littermates or infected adult dogs. The disease is usually fatal if contracted by puppies during the first three weeks of life. Older puppies with herpes virus usually have mild upper respiratory infections from which recovery is uneventful. Susceptibility of infant puppies is thought to be caused by their low body temperature. The canine herpes virus has been shown to multiply optimally at temperatures of 94° to 97°F, that of the neonatal puppy. It grows poorly at the body temperature of the adult dog.

The first symptom of affected puppies is soft, green odorless bowel movements. They may vomit or retch, have shallow respiration, which becomes gasping as the disease progresses, and refuse to nurse. They cry piteously and continuously.

Keeping puppies in a high environmental temperature for 24 hours is the only effective treatment; but even this is problematical. For three hours the temperature must be 100°F. The puppies need fluid to prevent dehydration, given orally every 15 minutes. Then the temperature can be reduced to 90°F for the remainder of the 24-hour period. If the puppies survive, the chances are better than average that they will live. Treatment is not advised if a puppy already has started to cry; this indicates that hemorrhaging has started and survival is doubtful; if it should live, chronic kidney disease may develop during the first year of life,

In kennels in which herpes virus is a recurrent problem, a preventive method is giving gamma globulin serum as an immunizing agent to neonatal puppies from dogs recovered from the disease. Since canine herpes virus is spread by direct contact with infected dogs, urine and other body secretions, overcrowding in kennels is a factor in disease transmission.

TOXIC MILK SYNDROME

Bacterial toxins in the bitch's milk caused by incomplete emptying of the uterus produce toxic effects in very young puppies (up to two weeks of age). Sick puppies cry, bloat, have diarrhea and red, swollen and protruding rectums,

They must be taken from the bitch, placed in a warm environment and given 5 to 15 percent glucose in water orally until the bloating has subsided. The bitch should be treated with appropriate medication to cleanse the uterus and antibiotics to prevent infection. The puppies can be put back with her as soon as treatment has started. They should be given a simulated bitch's milk product during the interval between glucose and water therapy and being returned to the bitch.

HEMORRHAGIC SYNDROME

Puppies have minimal production of a plasma protein called prothrombin during their first two or three days of life. Prothrombin is produced in the liver and, in conjunction with vitamin K_1, controls the clotting function of the blood. Without sufficient prothrombin, a hemorragic tendency can develop.

Affected puppies die within the first two or three days. They are lethargic, weak and decline rapidly in condition. Signs of hemorrhage may by lesions on the lips or tongue. Surviving puppies in the litter should receive Vitamin K_1. Most complete and balanced dog foods have sufficient vitamin K_1 for growth and maintenance of normal dogs.

CANINE PARVOVIRUS

Canine parvovirus has been recognized only since 1978 when epidemics were reported throughout the world. In 1979, the virus became a formidable disease in the United states. At that time, random studies revealed that between 20 percent and 50 percent of dogs tested had significantly high antibody titers suggestive of previous parvovirus infection. By the summer of 1980, new cases seemed to occur primarily among puppies under six months of age and in family pets that had not encountered the virus previously. Recent information indicates that while the over-all mortality of those dogs infected with canine parvovirus is less than 1 percent, the mortality among clinically ill dogs may be as great as 10 to 50 percent. These figures vary greatly among certain populations, since the severity of the disease appears to be influenced by such factors as crowding, age, and coinciding parasitic, protozoal infections. The incidence of the disease can be expected to decline as more dogs become resistant to the virus following infection or vaccination.

Canine parvovirus manifests itself in two distinct forms: enteritis and myocarditis. This section will concern itself only with the myocarditis form since it principally attacks puppies.

The myocarditis form occurs only in puppies born to a female who has no anti-bodies to parvovirus (one that has not had either the infection or current vaccination) and becomes infected with the virus during the first few days after giving birth. Lesions develop slowly in the puppies' heart muscles and heart failure is apparent several weeks later. The mortality rates in affected litters usually exceed 50 percent. Fortunately, the prevalence of the myocardial form already seems to be decreasing. The disease is due to the fact that many breeding bitches have been infected previously, and thus have circulating antibodies that are transferred to the puppies through the placenta and in the colostrum. This maternal antibody protects the newborns during their first five weeks when they are the most susceptible to the myocardial form of parvovirus.

Parvoviruses are especially hard to inactivate because they are resistant to heat, detergents, and alcohol. They have been known to remain active in dog feces, the primary source of infection, for more than three months at room temperature. A diluted (1:30) bleach solution is recommended for disinfecting because it will inactivate the virus. Since sanitation alone is not adequate to halt completely the spread of parvovirus, vaccination is the most effective method for control.

BRUCELLOSIS

Brucella Canis is relatively newly found and just recently recognized. Infections frequently become chronic. It occurs explosively and spreads rapidly among dog populations. The all prevailing nature of this disease under kennel conditions has been documented. One study found 86 percent of adult dogs became infected and 41 of 118 females aborted.

Although all breeds of dogs are susceptible and the disease is widespread in the U.S., reported incidence rates vary from one through six percent, depending upon the area samples (there seems to be a higher concentration in the South) and the type of diagnostic test employed.

Manifestations of Brucella Canis are similar to each of the other species of Brucella

In the bitches:

1. Infected females may abort their litters although without previous illness (typically in the final two weeks of gestation).

2. Pups born to infected mothers may be extremely weak; all or part of the litters may be stillborn.

3. Following an abortion, there is usually a discharge from the vagina lasting for several weeks.

4. Early embryonic deaths with termination of the pregnancy may occur, suggesting to the owner that the bitch failed to conceive.

Once the disease has been established in the male, the organisms are primarily transmitted venereally.

OTHER CAUSES

When confronted with neonatal puppy deaths, the breeder also should consider the possibility of other infectious canine diseases: distemper, leptospirosis, canine infectious hepatitis and the newest disease coronavirus.

Most puppy deaths are preventable with (1) selection of sound breeding stock, (2) a healthy, well-nourished bitch, (3) clean kenneling, (4) adequate heat for the bitch and the litter, (5) careful supervision of puppies' early weight gains, and (6) prompt veterinary assistance should puppies start to fade, cry, or have any of the early symptoms of puppy diseases.

CHAPTER 9

Analyzing a Pedigree

Anyone who has ever purchased a purebred dog has received a pedigree that, when used correctly, can be a real tool in breeding better specimens. It contains a list of names that usually go back to the fifth generation. Most newcomers have pored over their first pedigrees with great intensity, trying to sort out the infrequent *Ch.* preceding a dog's name. In addition, most pedigrees list the breeder's name, the date of birth, and the American Kennel Club registration number.

Unfortunately, most pedigrees, even those with many champions listed, have little meaning. A more meaningful pedigree would list the color of each dog (perhaps his/her measurements) and the number of champions produced. A picture of each dog in the first three generations would be of great help. To most owners, the list of names has little significance other than to highlight the champions of renown scattered through an otherwise nondescript pedigree.

As a list of the dog's forebears, the pedigree can be used by the wise breeder as a predictor of what kind of offspring the dog /bitch will produce. In effect, pedigree analysis is supposed to be able to help predict the next generation based upon previous generations.

That this is possible is true only in part. A good pedigree confirms what a dog's type and his proven ability to produce good stock have already proclaimed. The proof of the dog/bitch is in the puppies. The role of the ancestors is but a prelude to what is contained in the puppy's chromosomes.

It is a proven fact that an offspring of two parents who are themselves of high quality and are recognized producers of stock of consistent excellence, is likely to produce well.

Genetic research done by Francis Galton led to his so-called *Law of Filial Regression*, which states, in effect, the tendency of races to revert to mediocrity. This is what dog breeders refer to when they use the term *drag of the race.*

Galton reached his conclusions from statistical studies. He found that the adult children of very tall parents tended to be, while taller than the average of the population, not so tall as the mean height of the parents; and that the children of short parents tended to be shorter than the average but of greater height than the mean height of the parents. His statistics reveal the tendency of exaggeration of type in the parents to grow smaller or to disappear in the progeny.

In order to be a good breeder, one must use the pedigree as a basic record. A good breeder uses records to identify outstanding bloodlines possessing the ability to pass an animal's traits on to its progeny. Such bloodlines coupled with descriptive data — for example, a superior head — should constitute the information to be considered in planning a mating. In Europe, many breeders ask for the critiques done in the show ring on the dogs they plan to use for breeding. This gives them added objective information on which to make their breeding judgments.

Experienced breeders are able to prepare an intelligible pedigree, and as a result they can read meaning into a similarly prepared pedigree. Basically, however, most pedigrees are totally useless because they are incomplete and too often are only a jumble of names arranged in chronological order, linking one generation to the next. For most breeders, the pedigree could be written in Greek for all the good it does them.

Many breedings are well conceived and lead to the production of suitable specimens to carry on into succeeding generations. However, breedings of some famous dogs were made on a catch-as-catch-can basis.

A true story tells of the breeder who sent his nice bitch to a heavily campaigned and advertised stud dog. Now this dog was a sometimes breeder. If he didn't like the bitch, it was too bad. On this occasion he didn't take to the bitch and so ignored her. When the handler called the owner of the bitch to inform him, the owner said to breed her to any available stud since she would be out of season by the time he got her home to breed to another dog. This was done. From this chance mating came the top winning and producing dog in that breed's history. That such matings produce top specimens is more a tribute to Lady Luck than to the breeder's art.

There are wide differences existing in the gene structure of dogs, even from the same litters, and only a few specimens from any breeding can be outstanding as producers. Thus, the existence of famous names in a pedigree is not enough. It is no assurance whatever that the pedigree is a good one.

Good breeders follow the maxim of: "Every generation a good one." This means that each individual in a pedigree was a producer and that the line came down in a fixed series of progressions. It is not enough to have famous sires or dams spotted throughout the pedigree. It is necessary that their offspring were also producers so that the qualities of those famous dogs can be brought down to succeeding generations.

Each ancestor contributes to the heredity pool in its own unique way. Some improve upon the genes they receive while others degrade those qualities. A good bloodline is one in which each individual specimen has contributed to the *goodness* of the gene pool. Certain individual animals dramatically improve upon those characteristics, and it is these animals that should be perpetuated.

An outstanding pedigree shows an unbroken line of production in a form that a breeder can recognize immediately. Unfortunately, many a good pedigree has been turned into a poor one when one of the animals involved turns out to be an inferior producer (especially one close up) or a producer of serious faults. Unless each specimen is in turn followed by superior producers, it may reach a dead end for that line.

To have only a few good individuals in a pedigree is not enough. One has to appreciate that these individuals moved the breed toward the ideal. However, the ones to which they were bred may have carried genes detrimental to the breed, and, as a result, the influence of the noted producer may have been nullified.

While it is difficult for a modern breeder to assess the capability of any given dog or bitch in a pedigree to produce specific characteristics, he can be assured by an unbroken string of top producers that the gene pool is tending toward the overall ideal of the breed.

Livestock breeders have for many years recognized the necessity of maintaining an unbroken record of each line of ancestry. Voluminous computerized records are kept by the dairy cattle industry. Painstaking care is shown in selecting herd sires and keeping track of the milk and butterfat production of their offspring. The industry's ability to select proper specimens through computer analysis puts dog breeding to shame. The payoff in dollars is so great that this type of record keeping can be justified.

A great producing sire or dam produces a much higher average of good dogs among its progeny than does its less outstanding sons or daughters. When the great producing sire and the great producing dam are mated together, the average quality of the progeny is brought to its highest level. Even in this extremely favorable mating, however, the sampling nature of Mendelian inheritance and the range of natural variations would ensure that some of the offspring would be above and some below the average of the parents. In this case, the drag of the race would provide an entirely practical guarantee that the great majority of the offspring would be inferior as producers, to their great producing parents. Only the occasional one would be superior or even their equal.

With a pedigree that contains little but names, the older, more experienced breeder has an advantage, for he has undoubtedly seen many of the specimens listed. To the novice, pedigrees are to a large extent a mystery — a genealogical puzzle. The experienced breeder fills in from his own knowledge whatever he knows of the weighted averages of individuality and producing powers of each of the parents, the direct ancestors, and many collateral relatives. This is truly reading a pedigree, a gift of knowledge and insight which few breeders of any breed ever obtain.

The case of the newcomer is not so hopeless as it may seem, however. Before the usual pedigree can ever begin to become a reliable part of the basis of breeding, it is necessary to find out how superior or inferior each of the different ancestors was as a producer.

As pointed out earlier, progeny from superior sires and dams are more likely to be superior producers than the progeny of animals selected on the basis of individual merit and pedigree. However, it is sad to report that vast numbers breed to the winner of the day without regard for the genetic make-up of the dog. Perhaps that's why the average staying power of a breeder is only five years.

Progeny testing is invaluable for it reveals the true genetic make-up of the sires and dams. It is the heredity concealed in the genes of an individual that determines its value as a producer. All methods of arriving at the true nature of this heredity are merely estimates or approximations, except the actual testing in which this true nature definitely is revealed in the progeny itself.

The most accurate index of the breeding worth of sires and dams is the average quality of their offspring as a whole. In the absence of an ability to gauge this average accurately, the index lies in a random sample of the offspring rather than in the production of one super individual with the qualities of the other offspring unknown. As a consequence, a bloodline or a single mating that is known to produce a high average of good individuals must be considered a better bet. It offers more substantial assurances that a champion will be forthcoming in the next litter than one that has produced one champion but a lower average quality in all of the other offspring.

Experience has shown that the great mass of every breed fails to produce the required degree of excellence and is lost insofar as the perpetuation of the breed is concerned. The same principle applies to each line of ancestry, no matter how carefully the selections are made, and to the offspring of even the greatest sires and dams. It is common knowledge that the most *prepotent* sires of every breed have sired puppies that were inferior producers or even carried serious genetic faults. Thus it may be said that the purity of the line, even in the best appearing pedigrees, is no purity at all unless the progeny test can definitely be applied to each of the ancestors.

It is equally apparent that the mere appearance of famous individuals in a pedigree is not a sufficient guarantee that the line now retains any of those individual's good qualities, which may have been dissipated in their own or any succeeding generation by one or more inferior producers. To provide a reliable tool for the breeder bent on producing winners, the pedigree must show only lines of ancestors that are known to have a strong degree of purity for the sought-after qualities.

Decidedly more data is needed in most pedigrees. Until such data can be supplied, the short pedigree going directly to the superior producers is the best pedigree. Genetic research has shown that by far the greatest hereditary influence is exerted by the parents themselves, and that hereditary influence decreases rapidly in each more remote generation. Until tested, the most desirable breeding animal is one directly descended from known superior producers. Each intermediate generation of ancestors of undetermined or unknown breeding powers greatly lessens the probabilities of producing superior puppies.

PART III

All About the Border Terrier

- *The Standard of the Border Terrier*

- *Some Practical Aspects*

- *The Versatile Border Terrier*

- *The Working Border Terrier*

- *Obedience and Agility Competition*

- *The Border Terrier Around the World*

CHAPTER **10**

The Standard of the Border Terrier

Since the Border Terrier is a working Terrier of a size to go to ground and able, within reason, to follow a horse, his conformation should be such that he be ideally built to do his job. No deviations from this ideal conformation should be permitted, which would impair his usefulness in running his quarry to earth and in bolting it there from. For this work, he must be alert, active and agile, and capable of squeezing through narrow apertures and rapidly traversing any kind of terrain.

The Standard, in its introduction, sets forth what breeders, exhibitors, and judges must bear in mind at all times when viewing the Border Terrier: It is a working Terrier. Unlike many of the other breeds in the American Terrier group, which may make one wonder if their original purposes have been forgotten, today's Border Terrier remains similar in type to its rugged, game forebears that came out of the Border Country. Breeders on both sides of the Atlantic have tried very hard to see that it does not deviate from the original prototype. Many go-to-ground Terrier breed standards piously address themselves to the breeds' original purposes and functions. Yet, when one sees the reality of what the breeds have become in the show ring — sculpted and barbered, aggressive towards other dogs, and so big, thick, wide-chested, and barrel-ribbed that going-to-ground would be an impossibility — one realizes that such is not the case with the Border Terrier.

Before proceeding further with an explanation of the Standard, however, the phrase *built like a working Terrier* must be defined, for without an understanding of working conformation the ideal sought in the Border Terrier cannot be visualized.

First, foremost, and always to be remembered, is that a working Terrier must be narrow through the shoulder, chest, and rib-cage. This is applicable to all Terriers that are used for work. The true, working Terrier must go-to-ground and be able to get himself through the same hole in which his quarry disappeared. Moreover, once underground, the Terrier must be able to maneuver the twists and turns and then exit from his quarry's underground tunnel, burrow or hiding place. This last phase of the pursuit — getting himself out — is the most important. Anyone who has watched a Terrier in hot pursuit of his quarry knows that in the excitement and frenzy of the chase, many a Terrier has squeezed himself through apertures he might not otherwise have attempted. But when the Terrier has finished his work and is exhausted from the exertion, it is most important that his build allow him to turn around and exit easily.

For his work, the working Terrier must give the appearance of being narrow from all viewing angles. And, because a Border Terrier is a narrow, working Terrier, he must be capable of being spanned behind the withers by a man with average-sized hands. The show ring is not the place to ascertain a Border's working ability; it is, however, the place to determine if he is built to work. Any judge who evaluates the breed and awards championship points without spanning the entries is doing a disservice to the breed and has obviously not read the Standard. It can be stated unequivocally that a wide-chested, thick-shouldered, or barrel-ribbed Border Terrier is incorrect, and individuals of such type should end up at the bottom of their class's placings; they most certainly should not receive championship points.

The second of the two criteria for being a working Terrier as laid down by the Standard's introduction is that the Border Terrier must be able to follow a horse and rapidly cover ground in the pursuit of his quarry.

If breeders and judges are to remember that narrowness is the cornerstone for true working Terrier type, they must also bear in mind at all times that the Border Terrier must be up on leg able to meet the introduction's two requirements.

In short, as laid down by the introduction, the first impression of the Border Terrier is narrowness when viewed from front and top. This, coupled with sufficient leg, gives one the impression of a Terrier that can both successfully go-to-ground and rapidly cover any kind of terrain he meets.

Illustration 1. Ideal Border Terrier.

Illustration 1 is an example of a Border Terrier showing good length of leg, correct body proportions of height-to-body length, correctly set front, good rear angulation, and with a nice topline and proper tailset.

His head, like that of an otter, is distinctive, and his temperament ideally exemplifies that of a Terrier. By nature he is good-tempered, affectionate, obedient, and easily trained. In the field he is hard as nails, game as they come and driving in attack.

A discussion of the Border's head will be set aside for that section of the Standard in which it is described in detail. We state here, however, that the Border Terrier's head is an extremely important feature of the breed.

In the show ring, some people who are unfamiliar with the breed may be confused by the line in the introduction: "...his temperament exemplifies that of a Terrier." Because breeders are uniformly and correctly adamant about this aspect of the

Border Terrier, and because temperament is not mentioned elsewhere in the Standard, an explanation is needed at this point.

The Terrier temperament indicates a marked desire to have a go at the quarry — not other dogs. The Border Terrier is not quarrelsome towards other dogs. Under no circumstances should judges ever encourage Border Terriers to face off, spar or have a go at one another. Breeders have worked long years to maintain the original, true, working Terrier temperament, which is one that gets along with hounds and other Terriers. Indeed, true Border Terrier people would dismiss out of hand a quarrelsome, pugnacious individual and such an aggressive Border would have no place in a breeding program or in the show ring.

Those who have watched Border Terriers in the ring know they go about their business in a quiet and orderly fashion, while still exhibiting the characteristic "alert, active, and agile" demeanor called for in the Standard. The Border Terrier does have a sparkling, look-at-me presence, but this is achieved through his happy disposition and merry way of acting; he does not need to be sparked up or animated by challenging others of his breed to display his confident, steady nature.

It should be the aim of Border Terrier breeders to avoid such over emphasis of any point in the Standard that might lead to an unbalanced exaggeration.

We are fortunate that the Border Terrier has not passed through the tribulations of conformation exaggerations and fads that have beset other breeds of dogs. In large part, this is because the foundation stock of the breed was a naturally constructed, small, hunt Terrier. Unlike many breeds, the Border Terrier is a breed that does not lend itself to gross exaggeration; he does not possess an elongated head that can be over emphasized, unnaturally short legs on a normal-sized body, extremes of size — either giant or dwarf characteristics — nor does he possess extremely short-coupling that can lead to movement deficiencies. He stands four-square on legs of natural symmetry to his body size, and has dimensions of scope and range to allow for unrestricted movement and maneuverability. And while no breed of dog is completely lacking in some congenital problems, compared to other breeds of dogs, the Border Terrier has relatively few. The combination of the foundation Border Country stock being hardy, rugged, working Terriers and the fact that nothing about the Border's conformation lends itself to being overdone has given us today a healthy, natural, unspoiled breed.

GENERAL APPEARANCE — He is an active Terrier of medium bone, strongly put together, suggesting endurance and agility, but rather narrow in shoulder, body and quarter. The body is covered with a somewhat broken though close-fitting and intensely wiry jacket. The characteristic otter head with its keen eye, combined with a body poise that is at the alert, gives a look of fearless and implacable determination characteristic of the breed. The proportions should be that the height at the withers is slightly greater than the distance from the withers to the tail, i.e., by possibly 1-1 1/2 inches in a 14-pound dog.

The one point under General Appearance that is not found elsewhere in the Standard is the very last sentence of that paragraph. It would be interesting to know why this particular line was inserted in the U.S. Standard; generally, the U.S. Standard is an elaboration of the British Standard. But on this one particular point, the American Standard is in direct contradiction of the U.K. Standard. Regarding the issue of body and body proportions, the British Standard states simply: "Body: Deep and narrow and *fairly long*..." (authors' emphasis). It could be for this reason that U.S. Border Terrier people tend to ignore this part of their Standard.

No matter how one reads this line, however, and no matter what one's personal views are, there simply is no getting around the fact that in this sentence, the Standard is calling for a Terrier appearing square.

Let us say for illustrative purposes that a 14-pound dog is 14 inches at the withers (measuring directly down from the uppermost point of the dog's shoulder blades directly down his front legs to the ground). Adhering to the Standard, this dog then must measure 12 1/2 inches to 13 inches from the withers to the base of the tail.

Is this the height-to-length relationship that American Border Terrier breeders want? Emphatically, no! Those familiar with

Illustration 2. Too short-backed Border Terrier per the Standard.

Illustration 3. Correct body length-height proportions.

true breed type would say correctly that if these proportions prevailed, the Border would be too short-backed and lacking range and scope of body.

Illustration 2 shows a Terrier drawn to scale according to the American Standard's height-body-length requirement. It is decidedly an uncharacteristic, too short-backed Border Terrier. Illustration 3 more closely resembles correct body proportions that allow for maneuverability, scope and raciness.

When reading the Standard, both breeders and judges must also take into account the line that comes under the heading "BODY: Deep, fairly narrow and of sufficient length to avoid any suggestions of lack of range and agility." As Border Terrier people are aware, a short-backed dog simply would not have the flexibility and maneuverability when going-to-ground and attempting to twist and turn in a cramped and narrow earth. Additionally, movement anomalies occur when individuals are too short-coupled and have not the body length to accommodate the desired drive and reach. If we, at all times, bear in mind that a short back is not characteristic of the Border Terrier and is objectionable, we are on safe ground. The caution is that in obtaining the necessary length of body for range and agility, we achieve it through the thoracic area of the back rather than in the lumbar area, for an overly long loin area can lead to fatigue and weakness. See Illustration 4 for anatomical structure.

WEIGHT — Dogs, 13 - 15 1/2 pounds, bitches, 11 1/2 - 14 pounds, are appropriate weights for Border Terriers in hard-working condition.

There could be little argument that many Border Terriers in the ring today — on both sides of the Atlantic — tend to be larger than the weights stipulated in the Standard, and some of the winning Border Terriers are much bigger than the required weights. This dilemma, however, is nothing new and controversy as to size has been raging for as long as Borders have been in the ring and comments have been recorded.

Three factors are responsible for the discrepancy between what the Standard calls for and what is actually seen in the ring.

Illustration 4. Skeletal anatomy.

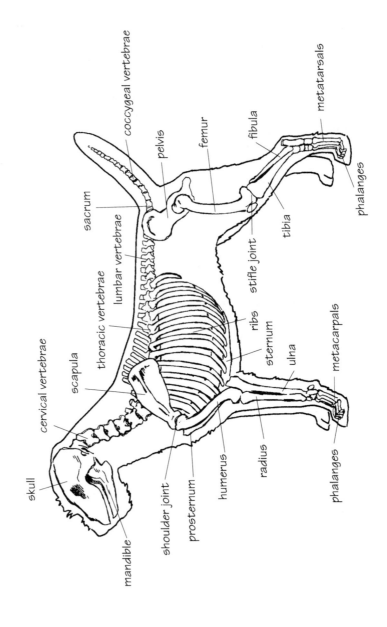

First, there can be little doubt that the nutrition breeders are able to provide Terriers today is far superior to what was available to the breeders who framed the Standard. Through better nutrition, statistics prove human beings have gotten bigger with each succeeding generation. There is no reason to assume that improved nutrition has not played a role in the increased size of Terriers.

Second, our weight requirements were borrowed from the British Standard. Traditionally, Britons maintain and show their Borders in a much thinner condition than do Americans. Some Americans, on the other hand, err in the opposite direction, and show grossly over-weight Terriers; neither rail-thin dogs, with ribs and hip bones clearly showing, nor gross obesity are to be desired. And, certainly, Americans cannot expect to have Terriers within the required weights if they persist in keeping and showing their Borders in an over-weight condition.

The third and final reason that many Borders seen in the ring are bigger than desired is the simple fact that breeders and exhibitors just don't pay enough attention to the required size.

One cannot have a Terrier that tips the scale at 18 to 20 pounds and have one that is narrow in shoulders and ribcage and can be spanned by a man's hand.

The Border Terrier has two distinctive features — hallmarks of the breed if you will. These are his otter head and his narrowness of body and front. When a specimen lacks one of these characteristics, he is devoid of one of the essentials of breed type.

HEAD — Similar to that of an otter. Moderately broad and flat in skull with plenty of width between the eyes and ears. A slight, moderately broad curve at the stop rather than a pronounced indentation. Cheeks slightly full.

The authors of the Standard most certainly had a head "like that of an otter" in mind, for this description is mentioned three times throughout the Standard.

But what, precisely, does an otter head look like? Let's assume we can rule out the sea otter (*Nutrias marinas*), as it is unlikely that Terriers from the United Kingdom would be compared to a mammal not found in its coastal areas.

Four other species can be ruled out: *Pternonura brasiliensis*, *amblonyx cinerea, Aonyx capensis, Paraonyx microdon, congica* and *philippsi* — none of which are Old World otters.

This leaves us with the river otter, *Lutra canadensis*. This otter is found throughout the world, and there are some 12 species. Apparently all are substantially the same in type.

Mammals of the World gives us this brief and puzzling head description: "The head is flattened and rounded" (Ernest Walker et al., The Johns Hopkins Press, Baltimore, 1968, Vol II, p. 1215 ft.).

Roger Caras, in *North American Mammals* (Galahad Books, N.Y., 1968, pp. 191-2), says the otter has: "Small eyes and ears, a broad, flattened head, a conspicuous nose pad, prominent whiskers" and, then later: "The river otter's eyes are located near the top of his head, to facilitate his seeing while cruising along almost totally submerged." Caras also states that the otter's sight and hearing are not exceptional, and that it relies on its sense of smell. So what about that " 'otter' head with keen eye?"

It is obvious from these descriptions that it was the general shape the Standard authors had in mind, for we most definitely do not want a rounded head, small eyes, or with eyes near the top of the head.

The general head shape of the river otter, *Lutra canadensis*, is one with a short, broad muzzle, and with a broad skull of good width.

Illustration 5 shows three examples of typical Border Terrier heads. Items *A* and *C* are good heads that demonstrate broad, flat skulls with well-filled muzzles, nice-sized ears that are level with the skull, and with expressions that have the desired "varminty" look. Item *B* is an example of an over-long muzzle with a foreign expression.

The Standard also calls for a moderately broad curve at the stop rather than a pronounced indentation. This does not seem to be a problem in the breed as a whole, and most individuals seem to display the correct amount of stop. The very few specimens with pronounced stop also possess disproportionately too-full cheeks and too-pronounced eyes, nearly buggy, which gives the entire head-piece an alien expression, somewhat like that of a Brussels Griffon.

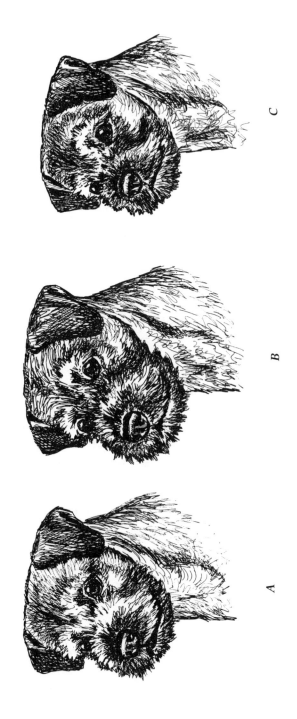

Illustration 5. Heads.

A

B

C

EARS — Small, V-shaped and of moderate thickness, dark preferred. Not set high on the head but somewhat on the side, and dropping forward close to the cheeks. They should not break above the level of the skull.

One would think that such relatively small features as the ears would be fairly unimportant in the overall conformation of the Border Terrier. Yet the first thing usually noticed about a dog is his head and expression, and it is remarkable how an otherwise very pleasing head and expression are ruined by incorrect ears.

The three most objectionable ear faults and the most prevalent ones are ears that are too large and "houndy," ears set too high on the head — giving the Border a strange, almost quizzical expression, and ears too light in weight that refuse to lie flat against the head, sometimes resembling a Whippet's called-for thrown back and folded ear.

With the first fault, overly large houndy ears, often the texture of the ear is thick, and nearly always, because of their thickness, they seem to lie correctly against the cheeks. Their size, however, not only can spoil an otherwise pleasing head and expression, but from a functional standpoint, provides more soft, fleshy area for injury from brambles as well as underground adversaries.

Similarly, high-set ears also detract from an otherwise good head and expression and give the Border a foreign look. While not set on as low as a Beagle's, for example, neither do they begin to approach the placement of a Fox Terrier's. A good rule of thumb is that when at the alert, with ears pricked, a good Border Terrier ear placement is level with the skull and should never break above this level.

The third and very prevalent ear fault is the too fine, folded fly-away ear. The very worst examples have nearly the classical rose ear.

All three ear faults are unquestionably hereditary results, for one can follow these faults through succeeding generations.

The Standard states that dark ears are preferred; dark ears undoubtedly complete the picture of a pleasing otter head and expression. As with so many other factors, however, in evaluating the Border, it is the dog's overall appearance that counts the most, and the *caveat* must be added to the Standard's preference for dark ears that this preference is given only with all other things being equal. One should not infer from the Standard that a faulty Border Terrier with dark ears is preferable to a better Terrier that has a bit lighter-colored ear.

EYES — Dark hazel and full of fire and intelligence. Moderate in size, neither prominent nor small and beady.

The authors of the United States Standard, for some reason, felt the need to expand on the British Standard in the description of the eye and eye color. The British Standard states simply about the eye: "Dark with keen expression."

It is unfortunate that the word *hazel* was added to the American Standard. In any dictionary the definition of this color is "light to strong brown or yellowish brown." Even with the Standard prefacing the word with *dark*, if interpreted literally, the Standard's requirement for any shade of hazel is a lighter colored eye than is truly desired.

The vast majority of the other Terrier breed Standards calls for eye color that ranges from *dark* and *very dark* to *as dark as possible*. And in the Border Terrier, it is the dark or very dark eye that gives the much desired varminty expression.

MUZZLE — Short and "well-filled." A dark muzzle is characteristic and desirable. A few short whiskers are natural to the breed.

As already mentioned, the Standard refers three times to the Border's head as resembling an otter. This section simply reinforces the idea that in aiming for the otter-like head, a short, well-filled muzzle is sought.

With the exception of a very few breed Standards, which give exact measurements or precise anatomical proportions in relationship to other anatomical components, most of the terminology in Standards — moderate, wide, long broad — is so imprecise as to allow for a great deal of individual interpretation. Such is the case also for *short* in the Border Terrier Standard, and which, in part, accounts for the many different muzzle lengths one sees in any large entry. *Short* is a relative term, first in relationship to skull size and breadth and in relationship to the Terrier's overall size and scope. Then, for judges and individuals unfamiliar with the breed, it is a relative term when compared with other Terrier breeds with which they are more familiar.

To add a bit more confusion to the discussion, some older breeders, especially in Britain, lament the fact that muzzles are becoming too short on the Border, although the British Standard similarly calls for a "short, strong muzzle."

Working Terrier enthusiasts jump into the fray, some saying that too short a muzzle endangers the eyes when the Border is in head-to-head or mouth-to-mouth combat with an adversary. Other working Terrier enthusiasts maintain with equal fervor that a short muzzle provides a more powerful, punishing grip and hold.

Thus, given the imprecision of the term short and the highly individual nature of breeding and showing, it is safe to say that the debate will never end.

There is no getting around the fact, however, that both the U.S. and U.K. Standards do require a short muzzle, regardless of the various arguments surrounding the issue. One is on safe ground if the relative proportions of one-third muzzle length to two-thirds skull length are kept in mind. An atypical, exaggerated Brussels Griffon head, which invariably leads to a foreign expression with buggy, glaring eyes and an upturned lower jaw, is as incorrect as the long-muzzled and long-skulled Fox Terrier heads so often seen in the ring.

There does not seem to be any argument, regardless of length, that the muzzle should be strong and well-filled. From directly under the eyes down to the nose, there should be no dropping away or chiseling as desired in some longer-headed Terrier breeds or most of the sight hounds. Thick or full muzzle whiskers may be deceiving in giving the appearance of a strong muzzle with good fill. In judging and evaluating a Border's head, one should gently grip and feel the muzzle as well as simply visually examining it. With the correct Border's head, the muzzle should feel like a good handful with plenty of breadth and no hint of weakness or snippiness.

As the Standard states, a dark-colored muzzle is characteristic, especially on the darker grizzled and deeper-colored specimen. The lighter-shaded reds tend not to have such dark-colored muzzles and as with dark ears, color considerations are always secondary to conformation and type.

TEETH — Strong, with a scissors bite, large in proportion to size of dog.

To those unfamiliar with the breed, invariably the very first statement uttered as they see a Border's teeth for the first time is: "My, what big teeth they have for dogs their size!" And that is precisely the impression one should get when looking at a Border's mouth. As working Terriers, they must have big, strong, functional teeth to grip and dispatch quarry. Small, undersized teeth, whether incisors, canines, or molars, are uncharacteristic of the breed. A scissors bite is one in which all of the upper incisors fit evenly and completely over the lower incisors. Anything other than this is not a scissors bite.

It is to the credit of the framers of the U.S. Standard that only a scissors bite is considered acceptable, for the British Standard states that a level bite is not only acceptable, but quite acceptable.

Neither Standard makes mention of one or several lower incisors incorrectly protruding and overlapping the upper incisors, a common occurrence in the breed.

Anyone with experience knows that Borders' teeth and jaws can continue to move, shift, and change as the dogs get older. The authors have seen any number of level bites in older Terriers shift to a reverse scissors and back to a level bite, as well as wry mouths shifting in adults to completely undershot bites and back to a wry bite. A good scissors bite however will seldom ever change. It remains a scissors bite. And a good scissors bite is one in which the upper incisors completely overlap the lower ones. Not just barely, but solidly and unquestionably. There have been reports of scissors bites changing and shifting. As with so many things in the dog world, however, it is a matter of definition and perception. One must question the type of scissors bite that changed; for if it were one in which the upper incisors barely covered the lower incisors, then one would indeed need to question if it was a good scissors bite in the first place.

The point of all this is that to accept anything less than a good, solid scissors bite in both the Terriers we show and the ones we breed is to invite trouble and simply perpetuate the mouth problems we have in the breed. It could, perhaps, be asked if we ever will eradicate mouth problems given the breed's fairly small gene pool. The only way we will make headway is to accept for ourselves only true, correct scissors bite.

NOSE — Black, and of a good size.

Little need be said about a Border Terrier's nose. Many years ago, a light-colored or liver nose may have occasionally appeared, but good pigmentation, including black noses, is now the norm.

In general, nose size and proportion in relation to the head are not a problem in the breed.

NECK — Clean, muscular, and only long enough to give a well-balanced appearance.
It should gradually widen into the shoulders.

SHOULDERS — Well laid back and of good length, the blades converging to the withers gradually from a brisket not excessively deep or narrow.

Because the neck of an animal and its shoulder assembly are so closely related to one another in overall conformation, neither can be adequately discussed nor explained without touching upon both. For that reason, this section of the Standard includes a concurrent examination of the neck region and the shoulders.

Usually, when one sees Terriers having the narrowness and raciness that are *de rigueur* for correct type, the over-all balance and neck length-to-body proportions are also correct.

Generally, when one sees a Terrier on which the neck does not look quite right, the problem most often tends to be the shoulder assembly of the individual, which tremendously affects both the appearance of neck length and the set-on of the neck (that is, how the neck blends into the Terrier's body and is set on the shoulders).

Perhaps the extremely oblique shoulder placement of sight hounds and trotting or cantering working breeds are not what's wanted on a Terrier that must both follow a horse *and* go-to-ground. Most certainly clean, efficient shoulders of sufficient lay-back that allow a Terrier to stay the course effortlessly on a day's hunt are wanted.

Straight shoulders invariably lead to two conformation problems relating to the neck, in addition to hindering the animal's efficiency of movement.

First, with the straight-shouldered animal, we encounter the individual that appears to have an overly short, out-of-proportion neck. It may not, however, be in the neck region wherein the fault lies, but in the shoulder placement; an animal with upright shoulders can often give the appearance of having a short neck. The second problem often encountered with straight shoulders is that the *set on* of the neck may be faulty. Frequently, it will appear as though the neck has been stuck on the body, and the lines of the neck and the lines of that part of the body where the neck comes into it will be at nearly abrupt angles, rather than having a nice, smooth blending of neck into the shoulder region.

Both breed characteristics and the anatomical requirements set forth by the Standard for Border Terriers were derived with the Border's working purposes in mind. As a powerful,

Illustration 6. Correct front assembly.

gripping jaw, handy size, and narrowness of scope serve the Terrier in its work, so too do good shoulders. Two dogs of approximately the same size, doing the same work, will expend equal amounts of energy doing that work. It is, however, that Terrier with well-laid shoulders who will cover more ground efficiently for the same amount of expended energy; and it is he who will out-last his straight-shouldered counterpart with his choppy, up-and-down front movement and lack of reach.

Finally, a discussion of the shoulder and front in the Border Terrier would not be complete without mentioning two other characteristics encountered too frequently in the breed. In addition to the straight shoulders encountered in the breed, over-developed, bunchy muscling over the shoulder blades too often is seen in Border Terriers. Not only are oblique, nicely laid shoulders to be desired, but so are flat, smooth, clean blades. When viewed from the front, the lines running down from the neck into the front legs should be smooth with no hint or indication of bunchiness in muscling or being loaded over the shoulders. This condition has little, if anything, to do with the amount of exercise a Terrier receives, for a Terrier with good, clean shoulders continues to have good, clean shoulders regardless of his work.

The other characteristic that is all too common is that in which the entire front assembly is placed too far forward on the body of the Terrier.

If an imaginary line were drawn straight down from the point of a correctly made Terrier's shoulder blades, that line would run approximately through the Terrier's front leg as seen in Illustration 6. Illustration 7 shows a Terrier with an all too-frequently seen front where the entire front assembly is set much too far forward on the body. Notice that the line falls behind the front leg.

Aside from aesthetics and a Terrier not looking quite right with an incorrectly placed front assembly, there is also a reason for having the front assembly under the dog rather than stuck on the front of the body. All dogs are held together by muscles and ligaments much more so than horses, which were some of the first animals on which movement was studied. The further forward on the body the front assembly is placed, the more strain is placed on the muscles and ligaments in movement and work, and more energy is required to do both. Additionally,

Illustration 7. Front assembly set too far forward on dog.

this fault is nearly always accompanied by too-steep shoulders and often with pinched fronts and random front movement. It is rare indeed to find a Terrier with well-laid shoulders possessing this front assembly fault.

FORELEGS — Straight and not too heavy in bone and placed slightly wider than in a Fox Terrier.

While the animal too heavy in bone is occasionally seen and to be avoided in a breeding program because of the accompanying thickness throughout that comes with too much bone, far more frequently it is the fine-boned animal lacking the endurance and substance for prolonged work that must be watched for. Medium is the only word to describe the proper bone needed on a Border Terrier, straying neither toward the big, cloddy specimens of massive bone, nor towards the pencil-legged, little weedy ones that pop up from time to time.

Equally important is straightness of limb. Those approaching a fiddle front in which the front feet and pasterns turn slightly outwards from the wrist down are not uncommon.

Illustration 8. Fronts.

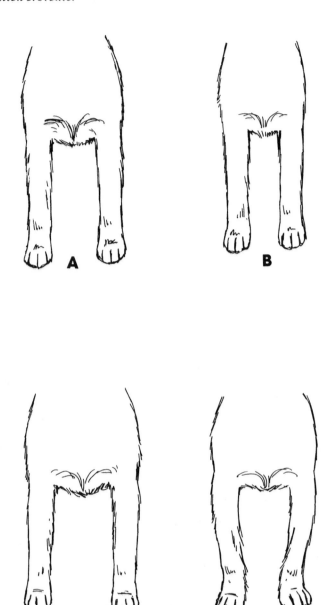

In keeping with his narrowness, the forelegs are not set wide apart. An exaggeration of this, however, wherein one finds fronts equally as narrow as Fox Terriers, or narrower, is to be avoided for it can lead to pinched fronts and front assembly movement problems.

Illustration 8 shows typical Border Terrier fronts. *B* is the ideal with correct narrowness of chest and shoulders. *A* is frequently seen and while not ideal, it is acceptable. *C* shows a front far too wide with the accompanying thick shoulders, and *D* is an example of a typical fiddle front with a slight bow in the front legs and turning out of the front feet. Varying degrees of this last fault are often seen, ranging from straight legs running down to the pasterns correctly with just the feet turning out to the front legs being even more bowed than in the illustration.

FEET — Small and compact. Toes should point forward and be moderately arched with thick pads.

For a working Terrier, his feet are some of his most important equipment, and unfortunately are all too often overlooked or ignored by judges in the show ring.

In size, they should be small, but in proportion to the dog's overall body make-up, and should give the appearance of being neat and tidy.

A cat foot may be fetching to some show enthusiasts, especially those unfamiliar with the breed. A foot, as described for a poodle for example — well-arched — is not, however, what's wanted on a working Terrier that must dig and scramble.

On the other hand, a splayed, flat, open foot is most certainly not desired, nor is a sight hound's hare foot. Rather, a moderately arched toe is sought, but strong, with no hint of weakness or breaking down. Equally as important, the pads should be thick and firm to give full protection to the underside of the foot.

At present, the two most common foot faults are large, over-sized feet that lend a lumbering, cloddy appearance to the bearers of such feet, and flat and splayed feet that would put a Terrier used for long periods of work at a disadvantage, if not eventually rendering him useless entirely.

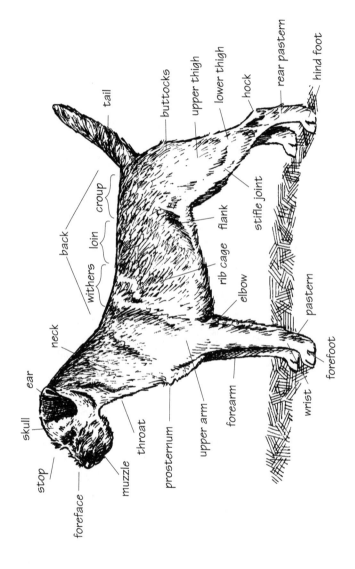

Illustration 9. External anatomy.

skull

ear

neck

stop

foreface

muzzle

throat

prosternum

upper arm

forearm

wrist

forefoot

pastern

elbow

rib cage

flank

stifle joint

withers

loin

croup

back

tail

buttocks

upper thigh

lower thigh

hock

rear pastern

hind foot

BODY — Deep, fairly narrow and of sufficient length to avoid any suggestion of lack of range and agility. Deep ribs carried well back and not oversprung in view of the desired depth and narrowness of body. The body should be capable of being spanned by a man's hands behind the shoulders, but laterally supple, with no suspicion of a dip behind the shoulder. Loin strong and the underline fairly straight.

Regarding the length of the body, the Standard requires that there be sufficient length to avoid lack of maneuverability and agility. The British Standard goes even further in this direction by asking for a body that is fairly long. While a discussion of back length appeared above under *General Appearance*, the concern stated there bears repeating, and is so stated in the Standard. Too often the required scope or length is found in the lumbar vertebrae area (the loin area) rather than in the thoracic vertebra above the rib-cage area. It was precisely this concern the Standard framers had in mind when they stipulated that the "ribs (are to be) carried well back..." This question of an overlong loin region logically leads into a brief comment on one of the breed's biggest bugbears today: faulty toplines. (Technically, topline refers to the line running from behind a dog's ears to the base of his tail; backline refers to the line from a dog's withers to the base of the tail, and it is to this latter area we address ourselves. Common U.S. usage, however, adopts the term topline for backline.)

The only line in the Standard that refers to the Border's topline is: "Back strong but laterally supple, with no suspicion of a dip behind the shoulders." And the abbreviated British Standard makes no mention of it at all.

Frankly, there is every good reason to try for level toplines in Border Terriers. Why be concerned at all about toplines? After all, does a Terrier's topline affect his working ability? The answer is yes, in the same indirect way that sound movement serves a working Terrier well. If one thinks of a dog's movement in elementary engineering terms, he has "x" amounts of energy; this energy originates in the angles and levers of his rear quarters (his drive), is transmitted along a line (his spine), and is imparted to the angles and levers of his front assembly (his reach) which pulls and guides this energy along, if you will.

A well-put-together animal has no wasted movement or energy. And a straight line (i.e., level or straight being the most common terminology used in other breeds' Standards) of the spine is the most efficient in transmitting energy. It was not for esthetic purposes that the writers of the Standards for Airedales, American Staffordshires, Australians, Cairns, Fox Terriers, Irish Terriers, Kerries, Lakelands, Schnauzers, Norwichs, Skyes, Soft-Coated Wheaten Terriers, Staffordshire Bull Terriers, and West Highland Whites all require a level or straight topline. It is because it's the most efficient topline in a Terrier. Good, solid, level toplines are part of good, sound movement; all the anatomical parts of the Terrier including his topline serve him when he is on the move. And most definitely, a topline can be solidly level while being simultaneously supple.

There are varying theories regarding the presence of a dip behind the shoulders somewhere between the fourth and sixth thoracic vertebrae. Many breed Standards, including the Border's, require that there be no dip present. On the other hand, some who have made an in-depth study of canine movement insist that the dip must be present to have a properly moving dog. Some, in fact, for reasons unfathomable, have gilded the lily and given it a German name, which, when translated into English, means dip. Regardless of one's choice of languages, the debate continues and there is no good reason to take issue with the authors of our Standard on the point.

The last point mentioned under the heading of *Body* is that the underline should be fairly straight. While there does not seem to be a problem with this in the breed to any great extent, one does very occasionally see a Terrier that is tremendously cut up in the flank, with the underline somewhat resembling a Whippet's. Almost always, however, these Terriers that are quite cut up in the flank also tend to be those extreme in type and lacking in substance, resembling a Whippet not only in amount of cut up, but also in bone and body proportions as well.

TAIL — Moderately short, thick at the base, then tapering. Not set on too high. Carried gaily when at the alert, but not over the back. When at ease, a Border may drop his stern.

Repeated often enough as to be trite, the analogy of a carrot is too apt not to be stated here in describing the sought-after tail in the Border. And, as with the entire conformation of the Border, this moderately short, good, strong tail is functional: more than one Border has been pulled from an earth by this handy appendage!

Long, thin, whip-like tails are anathema and are to be strenuously avoided in any breeding program. As with an extreme cut-up in the flank and the often accompanying Whippet-like type, very often Borders possessing a very long, thin, whip-like tail tend to be over long in the length of the lumbar vertebrae region, foreface, skull, and length of leg in body-leg proportions.

The set-on of the tail is one of the very few characteristics in which there is a marked difference between the U.S. Standard and the British Standard, although the rationale for the alteration in the expanded U.S. Standard is unclear. Whereas the British Standard requires a tail set high, the American Standard stipulates a tail not set on too high.

While this difference may appear small at first glance, the danger of a tail set not too high is that a low tail set could be inferred as being correct, and dogs bred accordingly.

The tail is the final portion of the spine and is composed of the coccygeal vertebrae; its placement is dependent on the manner in which it is attached to the sacral region of the spine (which lies at the end of the croup just above the pelvis bone). If caution is not used and an eye not kept to it, in an attempt for a tail set not too high, the entire rear assembly can be thrown off. As all skeletal components are integral to a dog's movement, so, too, are the components of a dog's rear, including the relationship of the sacral region, coccygeal vertebrae region, and the pelvis. If, in fact, an overly low attachment of the coccygeal vertebrae to the sacrum is sought, the angle of the pelvis, itself, can be incorrectly altered. And, if the angle of the pelvis becomes too steep, the entire rear assembly is thrust under the dog and too far forward, which then renders the dog incapable of any sort of drive from his rear quarters. He, in fact, travels under himself on the move. Unfortunately, this phenomenon of a steep pelvis and a dog traveling under himself in the rear is seen far too commonly in the ring. Visually, when the dog is standing, this steep pelvis construction manifests itself in a goose rump and its accompanying lack of muscle development, or a steep croup that falls away.

Regarding tail carriage, technically, a gay tail or one carried gaily is one that is carried higher than the horizontal. As the Standard stipulates, however, it cannot be carried over the back. Thus, correct tail carriage in the Border Terrier on the move can range from high noon (straight up) to three o'clock (horizontal).

Along the same line, the angle at which a Border's tail is held by the handler when being examined by the judge or for a picture has also been misunderstood. Traditionally, in all breeds the tail is held by the handler at the angle at which the dog naturally carries it when on the move or at the alert. Yet, somehow, for even a Border with an upright tail, to Border Terrier people it never looks quite right when the tail is held at a 90° angle for examination or picture. Consensus seems to be that a tail held at approximately a 45° - 47° angle seems to present the most pleasing picture. It is again surprising at the number of examining judges unfamiliar with the breed who will either thrust the tail into an upright position, or who will be adamant that the tail be stretched out horizontally in setter-like fashion.

Finally, it is natural that the Border not carry his tail up all the time as do some of the other Terrier breeds. Usually, it is only when he's moving or at the alert that the Border's tail is up. For judges to penalize exhibits that drop their tails when standing at ease or baiting is to misunderstand the breed.

HINDQUARTERS — Muscular and racy, with thighs long and nicely molded. Stifles well bent and hocks well let down.

The given in examining a Border Terrier's hindquarters is that one seeks the structure for good drive and the maximum efficiency to achieve this drive. It is then a small jump in thought to realize that to achieve this drive (or push or propelling thrust) from the hindquarters, the longer the dog's thighs, the greater potential he possesses to thrust energy into his hocks, which in turn transmit this energy into his foot, which then propels him forward. With good length and muscular development of the upper and lower thighs, quite simply put, the dog has more with which to begin the propelling process. Combined with this — as the Standard requires — the stifle must be set at the correct angle "well bent" so that the energy traveling along the upper thigh is transmitted towards the dog's rear, rather than down as is the case when the stifle angle is slight. With an insufficient angle where the femur and the tibia-fibula converge (the stifle), the dog is, in fact, quite literally pushing more into the ground directly beneath him, than pushing in a rear direction. This, then, accounts for the fact that when one observes straight-stifled individuals (in which the stifles are not well bent) they do not seem to be covering much ground or to be going anywhere. Rather than pushing themselves forward, they are pounding the ground in an up-and-down fashion, nearly having to pick up the entire rear assembly and moving it forward in a stilted, choppy fashion.

Further, once this propelling thrust has reached the hock, the shortest route to the foot and then to the ground would seem to be the most efficient. And it is! That is precisely the reasons the framers of the Standard stipulated "hocks well let down." The closer the hocks are to the ground, the shorter the rear pastern will be, and thereby the shortest route to the pushing-off foot will be accomplished. Thus, with good length of thighs, a sufficient stifle angle, low hocks, and a short rear pastern, the dog is able to maximize his energy into propelling himself forward in smooth, fluid motion. With both correct angles and the correct levers, the rear is, indeed, a most efficient driving apparatus.

COAT — A short and dense undercoat covered with a very wiry and somewhat broken top coat which should lie closely, but it must not show any tendency to curl or wave. With such a coat a Border should be able to be exhibited almost in his natural state, nothing more in the way of trimming being needed than a tidying-up of the head, neck and feet.

As with all of the hard-coated Terrier breeds, the Border has a double coat that serves him well in all kinds of weather. A good, hard, wiry outer coat repels water, burrs, and dirt that would cling to a coat with a softer texture. Beneath this perfect working jacket, as indicated by the Standard, is a thick, velvet-like undercoat next to the skin that tends to be water repellent and keeps in the dog's body warmth. Mother Nature in her wisdom provided the Border with one of the best coats imaginable for a working Terrier. It is therefore imperative that the Border possess both coats, and that the outer coat is the right sort of harsh, wiry texture.

It is safe to say that the Standard in describing a coat that needs but tidying up about the head, neck, and feet is setting down a blueprint for the ideal Border Terrier coat, which of course Standards are supposed to do. Indeed, the prescribed coat is the sort all breeders would dearly love to get their hands on, or perhaps more accurately, the type they would not have to put their hands on. Unfortunately, the reality of many Border Terrier coats today is that they are not quite as described above, and the majority do need to have the entire body periodically stripped out. Saying this, it should be the aim to try to for the rare coats that never need to be stripped and even with coats that tend to grow over-long and need to be stripped out, the hard, wiry texture must be present.

As an aside, frankly it must be questioned just how many of the early U.S. Border Terriers did possess the coat as set forth in the Standard. As anyone who has seen a Terrier with the extremely hard, always-neat type coat knows, the few short whiskers that are natural to the breed range from the very short to the non-existent. To achieve this sort of coat, the texture must be of the very harshest, and this harshness extends to the whiskers; whiskers of this type are, in fact, so harsh that they never grow to any length because they break off. It is impossible to have a face full of whiskers while at the same time having an ideal, no-strip kind of coat. Pictures of the earliest American dogs indicate that only a handful had coats of the ideal sort as most tended to have a full complement of face whiskers.

Stating the above, it must be quickly added that in mentioning whiskers on the muzzle, a schnauzer-like abundance is not desired. Since the authors' earliest days in the breed, there have always been a few who have tried with grooming to make the Border into something he is not. While the subject of grooming, itself, will be addressed in another section of this book, suffice it here to say that in regard to whiskers on the muzzle, a look of fullness of muzzle should be the aim of the whiskers present rather than a long, over-abundant, goat-like beard. Anything but a few whiskers that enhance the Border's full muzzle and otter-like head give him a decidedly atypical look and expression.

Given the prevalent type of coat found on the majority of Borders today, one walks a fine line in achieving the coat described in the Standard. First of all, it asks for a "somewhat broken top coat." It is a bit difficult describing in words the exact meaning of broken, as applied to Borders. Some authorities apply the word to all Terrier breeds in general, and define it as wiry or harsh or crinkly (as one would find the coat of a Wirehaired Fox Terrier to be). Yet for Border Terriers, the meaning goes beyond this. Most certainly, a crinkly coat is not what's sought. Probably the best synonym would be tweedy, for when looking at a good Border coat in its prime, the picture of a woolen tweed jacket comes to mind; with the colors of the Border's coat — whether a red, grizzle, or blue-and-tan — there is always an intermingling of various shades of the colors on the same dog, which in addition to the texture, enhances the tweedy appearance of the coat. Moreover, when the coat is long enough to achieve the tweedy look, the individual hairs seem to group together to add shadings and highlights to the coat color. Generally, this broken or tweedy appearance is not attained until the coat is about one and one-fourth inches to one and one-half inches in length.

In addition to the requirement for a broken coat, the Standard states that the coat "should lie closely." Unfortunately, some exhibitors remember only one part of the Standard's sentence and forget the other; neither an open, blown coat, nor an extremely short coat (skinned as some would call it) is the aim. No doubt the AKC's slide show on the breed stated it best when it recommended that when shown, a Border's coat should be of sufficient length so that its texture can be adequately evaluated.

HIDE — *Very thick and loose fitting.*

The hide or pelt of the Border Terrier is another individual characteristic found in few other breeds, and again of a functional nature. For protection against bites and scratches, it is imperative the Border's hide be thick and tough. Equally as important as its thickness, the hide should also be loose and pliable. The hide is so loose, in fact, that many an old-timer in the breed or a huntsman has been seen to pick a Border up by the pelt to test it, with no apparent pain or alarm to the Terrier. The looseness of the hide, of course, allows the Border to squeeze easily through any narrow openings he may encounter while working.

MOVEMENT — Straight and rhythmical before and behind, with good length of stride and flexing of stifle and hock. The dog should respond to his handler with a gait that is free, agile, and quick.

Throughout this discussion of the Standard, the Border's conformation as it relates to its work has been repeatedly stressed. And, as it has been alluded to, the proof of the pudding as to how a dog is put together is his movement. When correctly made, the Terrier moves straight from the ground up with no wasted motion in feet, front pasterns, front legs, elbows, hocks, or rear pasterns. In addition to trueness coming and going, the Standard requires good reach in front (good length of stride) and drive in the rear (flexing of stifle and hock).

Finally, there is nothing ponderous or hesitant in the correctly made Border on the move; shown on a loose lead, he indeed moves out in a manner that is "free, agile, and quick."

COLOR — Red, grizzle and tan, blue and tan, or wheaten. A small amount of white may be allowed on the chest but white on the feet should be penalized.

It is not inappropriate that when the Standard was drawn up, color was the last characteristic to be listed. To most long-time, experienced Border Terrier people, color is of such little importance that it is the last consideration, if considered at all. Granted, there is nothing more eye-fetching than a well-made Border Terrier carrying a deep, rich, red jacket; some breeders may have a slight preference to a well-made blue and tan, but the emphasis of knowledgeable breeders is always on the well-made aspect of that statement. Color does not have the least bearing on either a Border's conformation or his working ability.

Similarly, there should be no prejudice by judges in the show ring regarding color; the colors as they are stated in the Standard are not in order of preference, but are merely a listing of the colors found in the breed. At one time, it may have been a bit more difficult to finish a blue and tan in the U.S., but then perhaps the quality of blue and tans years ago was not quite up to that of the reds and grizzle and tans. All that has changed, however, and many good quality blue and tans seen in the ring today finish their championships handily.

While it is not our intention to delve deeply into a discussion of coat color as it is a fairly minor consideration in the breed and has been well handled in other publications, a *caveat* must be inserted regarding blue and tan. They are just that: blue. They are not black and tan as seen in other Terrier breeds. With age and maturity, a proper blue and tan appears decidedly blue with silver hairs liberally interspersed among the darker hairs. Adults with a deep black body showing no sign of silver and with Irish Terrier or Irish Setter red rather than tan are not blue and tans and are not mentioned in the Standard. Wheaten is listed as a color in the Standard, although it is the consensus that a true wheaten is not to be found today. A wheaten is the same color as a Soft-Coated Wheaten Terrier with no grizzling, and with a bluish cast in its ears. Occasionally, one hears of a Border being called a wheaten, but on examination, it will be found to be a very light red.

Very often, the color of pups at birth can be misleading, because many, especially the reds, are born so dark as to be nearly black. By examining the hairs on the back of the skull, one can ascertain if the pups will be reds or grizzles or if they will be blue and tans; the reds and grizzles will have few brownish-red hairs, while the blue and tans will appear solidly black. Week by week after birth, the various shades of reds and grizzles will progressively lighten and will mature a much lighter color than they were at birth.

Interestingly, the color of some mature dogs may vary somewhat from stripping to stripping and from coat to coat. While this variation does not change a red into a grizzle and tan or vice versa, there are changes in shade of the basic color, and often one coat will be somewhat more or less grizzled than a previous one. When diet and all environmental factors remain constant, and variations still occur, one cannot help wondering if length of daylight hours and temperature do not play some role in these subtle coat-color changes. The reasons, however, are mere speculation.

CHAPTER 11

Practical Aspects

CHOOSING A PUPPY

Selection of a puppy, particularly one of show quality, is something of a gamble. The puppy that may appear as pick of the litter at a tender age can develop major faults as he matures (which, however, will not interfere with his qualities as a pet or obedience prospect). This said, here are some points to look for in choosing a Border Terrier.

Most important is temperament. Avoid puppies that back off from you, cringe, or sit back unresponsively. Shyness may be due to heredity, or to lack of socialization. Whatever the cause, it is to be avoided.

Wilson Stephens, writing in the English magazine, *The Field* (February 7, 1979), put it well:

> In all terriers, whether operationally employed or family companions, temperament is a prime consideration. Unlike pastoral breeds, terriers have no strong guarding instinct, beyond that conferred by loyalty to their owners, and built-in high spirits...
>
> Reliable temperaments are most often found in breeds associated with the less wealthy communities, and with not too long standing a popularity as show dogs ... (show people) whose dogs have been kept in kennels for generations, can tolerate doubtful temperaments in animals which have compensating qualities, or even remain in ignorance of them. But one-bitch breeders with a household where litters are whelped and reared in

that best of all environments, under the kitchen table, will not long endure an animal which does not command universal popularity.

Show-ring temperament too often means the animal is showy and fiery in the ring, but may have unsuitable behavior at home, when exhibiting is the prime consideration. It should be noted here that Borders are not expected to be aggressive when shown, or be made to spar.

A few simple tests can be used when looking at a litter, such as clapping your hands, dropping a feed dish, tossing a ball, or rolling the puppy over on his back. The normal puppy may be startled at any of these activities, but will bounce right back. Such tests will help spot the nervous, timid, or unduly aggressive dog.

It is difficult to evaluate with certainty a puppy from the standpoint of conformation before he is eight to ten weeks of age. Before that period, he's simply too young, and after that the puppy enters the awkward and leggy state. But, during these two critical weeks, it is possible to tell what the dog will look like at maturity — any faults will carry over to the adult age.

Beginning with the head, there are points to look for and to avoid. Most puppies' heads are appealing for the first five to six weeks. After that, faults such as a narrow skull and "snipey" muzzles will show. Look for good width between the eyes, with good breadth of skull and muzzle. At eight to ten weeks, the head is much as it will be in proportion at maturity. Ears should be set low and small, and there should be a good reach of neck.

The bite can be one of the Border Terrier's biggest problems. Look for a good scissors bite and avoid a puppy that has a level or undershot bite with the first teeth. The more space between the upper and lower incisors, the better. Unfortunately, there is absolutely no guarantee that an excellent bite in a puppy will develop correctly as the second teeth come in. This is one factor no reputable breeder will guarantee: bad bites are endemic in Borders and completely unpredictable.

Check for good bone. A fine-boned puppy will always be fine-boned, a most undesirable trait. The topline must be level — at this stage of evaluation you may be sure that any faults will continue and not improve or disappear. A correct topline at this point may go off as the puppy develops, but it will be a temporary variation and should be level at maturity.

Look for a short, thick carrot-like tail. It should not be low set, but should be a continuation of the spine. It must be straight, with no kinks.

Overall, the young Border should stand squarely, with well-bent stifle and nicely laid-back shoulder. Straight stifles and shoulders will not improve with age.

Finally, the coat should be hard and wiry, with no indication of softness or fluffiness, and should be hard to the touch. The coat beneath must be checked for correct quality, and the beginning of a good undercoat should be apparent. There should be no white on the toes, but a very small white spot on the chest is permissible, although not preferred.

As to breeding, whelping and veterinary care, there are many excellent books that cover such matters in detail. New publications are constantly being issued, and for information on such topics, refer to them and to your veterinarian. Above all, don't rely on old-wives' tales or off-hand advice from your neighbor.

However, there are certain aspects of rearing and care of the Border Terrier that should be mentioned here, including the important topic of grooming.

REARING THE PUPPY

As emphasized in the above section, temperament is extremely important. The Border Terrier's nature is quite unlike that of other Terriers. Originally bred as a hunt Terrier to be used with a pack of hounds, the Border had to get along with other dogs. This has resulted in a Terrier that is not aggressive or belligerent. But varmints are another matter. The Border will enthusiastically tackle small game, such as rats, woodchucks, squirrels and so on. Although the majority of the breed in the United States is not used for working, there is an active Working Terrier Association, and the role of the Border in Working Trials is discussed in full in Chapter 13.

A word of caution: Borders will live peacefully with cats if they are brought up with felines, otherwise one must take care. Also, males will occasionally fight with other males.

All dogs need socialization, and perhaps the Border requires more than some other breeds. What is socialization? It is exposing the puppy to all sorts of situations, people, and places. All this must be done in his early life, the first 12 weeks being the most critical. At that time the puppy's reactions to various stimuli are set for the remainder of his life. Isolation in a kennel, or lack of contact with other dogs and people will result in an adult who may be shy, aggressive, or intractable.

Borders are sensitive. Harsh training will break a happy, playful puppy's spirit. Firm but gentle treatment is the key, and will produce excellent results, while yelling and scolding will be disastrous. Hitting a puppy is deplorable and completely unnecessary.

The puppy must learn to obey, however. Reward good behavior and discourage bad habits. For example, if the dog chews on something he shouldn't, such as a shoe or the furniture, reprimand him firmly, but gently. Then present him with something suitable to chew on, such as a rawhide toy or *Nylabone.*

Always reward good behavior and discourage bad — we repeat this because of its great importance.

The problem that seems to worry new owners the most is house training. We avoid the term house *breaking,* as that implies harsh methods and coercion. Bear in mind that for the first 10 to 12 weeks of his life, the puppy does not have complete control of his elimination. But most accidents can be avoided by careful attention and frequent trips outside. After each feeding, take the Border out, and praise him very enthusiastically when he performs. If he does relieve himself in the house, do not, repeat do not, spank or otherwise punish him. Be patient. If the pup seems restless, wanders around and puts his nose down, take him outside immediately as those are signs of necessity.

Many owners find the use of a crate helpful. A crate with puppy's blanket and a few toys will soon become his home, where he can be left for short periods. However, do not leave the Border for long stretches of time in the crate: The object is to make it a special spot for the puppy, a retreat, not a prison. The secret is always to make the crate an enjoyable experience. It is never used as a punishment. Give lavish praise or a treat each time the dog is put in his crate. Most puppies adapt very happily to the crate, and it makes housetraining easier, as a puppy will not soil its bed if it can be helped.

In any case, relax about housetraining. Border Terriers are clean little dogs, and eventually the problem will be solved. Again, patience is the key.

Puppies should be checked for parasites: round worm, hook and others. A regular schedule of preventive shots should be arranged with your veterinarian. Methods and routines constantly change, so for the latest developments, consult the vet.

FEEDING THE PUPPY

Feeding the Border Terrier puppy is quite simple. When the puppy is obtained from the breeder, directions will be given to the new owner, so there won't be any upsets due to change in diet. If the breeder does not volunteer instructions, the new owner must ask for them. Be prepared for a few upsets, however, as the change in environment, as well as in water, will cause some temporary difficulties, such as diarrhea, in many puppies. Normally, a young dog is fed twice a day, taken outdoors and allowed to eliminate a few minutes after eating, then given a rest period.

As the puppy grows, the amount of food given should be increased. As a general rule, feed 30 calories per pound of dog for adults, slightly more for puppies. Your puppy should not be fat, nor should he be so skinny that his ribs and hip bones show.

Avoid generic or cheap grocery store brands of dry food. Stick to a good quality that states clearly the ingredients and caloric value. However, do not follow the amounts to feed as given on most packages, as each dog is different, and you will learn to adjust accordingly.

A caution: Never change feed suddenly. If it is necessary to switch, make the change very gradually. This is true for adults as well as puppies. Do not feed milk, as it is completely unnecessary. Never add supplements, particularly calcium or vitamins (unless prescribed by your veterinarian).

Under general care, there are attentions that should be paid to any breed of dog. These include, to begin with, clipping the toenails. If one starts when the puppy is very young, and one is extremely careful not to injure the sensitive nail or frighten the animal by holding too tightly, normally the Border will accept this as a regular event. There are various types of nail clippers: The most popular is the *guillotine*, in which the nail is inserted into a small hole. These are available at any pet or general store, but buy good quality, as some clippers are cheaply made and will pinch instead of cutting cleanly.

Ears should be checked for cleanliness or other problems, such as burrs or ticks. The anal area must be inspected. Your veterinarian can take care of difficulties with anal glands, which in some dogs become impacted. If your dog scoots or rubs his rear end, it is not a sign that he has worms (an old wives' tale), but that he probably needs the anal glands expressed. If you wish to perform the process yourself, have your vet teach you, but it's messy and odorous.

Eyes, too, normally cause no problems, although some may *tear* and need to be wiped, an attention many dogs require. Teeth must be regularly checked and tartar removed as needed.

The Border Terrier is fortunately not as susceptible to skin ailments as some other Terrier breeds, and is generally happy and healthy.

The coat is the main factor in Border up-keep. Yes, the breed sheds. Yes, the coat does require care, but far less than that of most Terrier breeds. Bathing should be avoided, as the Border's tough and wiry coat may be softened by the process.

The breed Standard specifically states: "A Border should be able to be exhibited almost in his natural state, nothing more in the way of trimming being needed than a tidying-up of the head, neck and feet."

The coat does, however, need to be stripped at least twice a year, a process that is time consuming, but not painful to the dog. It consists of removing the top coat, which is rather wiry and heavy and can grow so long that the dog looks quite bushy and ragged. The term *blown* is used when the top coat is overlong and ready to shed. The dead hairs are removed by a process called stripping, and it does take time.

The owner can use fingers, in which case the old dead hair is pulled out in small amounts, always going with the direction of the hair. The greatest care should be taken when doing sensitive areas, such as ears, rear, and belly.

The owner may prefer to use a stripping comb, in which case one should be found with a handle that fits the owner's hand comfortably. Again, go with the way the hair lies, using the comb and thumb to remove the lifeless hair.

Tidying means just that, stripping off extra hair on the feet and around the ears. Do not remove all the hair on the Border's face. Some have more whisker and eyebrow hair than others and can benefit by a little extra neatening. Try to have an experienced person show you the skills of coat care. After stripping, only the undercoat will remain.

It should take about two months after a dog sheds out and is stripped for the coat to grow out again. There are also considerable variations in coat within the breed. Some will shed out naturally and the lucky owner need only brush the dog regularly. Others are very easy to strip and seem to enjoy the attention. There are some, unfortunately, who don't take kindly to the process and whose coats are difficult to take down. Regular brushing and combing between major grooming is important, and will also alert the owner to possible flea and tick infestations, or other problems.

Ch. Hollybridge Raffles, VDT, CG on the hunt, 1991.

CHAPTER 12

The Versatile Border Terrier

One of the outstanding traits of the Border Terrier is its adaptability. It's a wonderful house pet and companion with friendly and appealing ways. Normally, it isn't aggressive with other pets, and this may include cats if it's accustomed to them from puppyhood. The Border Terrier is astonishingly versatile.

The breed is tireless and plucky as a hunter. This aspect of the Border is described in the chapter: *The Working Border Terrier*, written by enthusiast Barbara Kemp of Steephollow Kennels. In the field, the Border will tackle anything, regardless of size or ferocity. This may lead to wounds and battle scars; the sport is not for the faint of heart or squeamish owner, but most Terriers have the instinct and adore hunting.

Not too many owners have gone in for the tracking dog degree (TD), an AKC-recognized sport, but it is great fun for Borders and they enjoy it. In 1972, Nancy Hughes's *Ch. Chief of Lothian, CG UDT* (Wharfholm Whipperin x Ch. Rose Bud of Lothian, bred by Mrs. H. Pettigrew) was the first of the breed to win the degree. Since then, more than 15 Borders have become TDs and there is at least one TDX, *Dickendall's Heartstopper* (Ch. Polydorus Pookoo x Ch. Dickendalls Heartbreaker, bred by Kendall Herr and co-owned with Susane Berman). She achieved this in 1987 when she was less than three years old.

As for obedience, more than 225 Borders have become companion dogs (CD), 66 have qualified as CDX, and 23 as UDs. These figures are through 1990 only, so many more will have earned titles since then. The second Border to win an Obedience Championship was *Ketka's Fine O'Pinyon*, who also holds the Canadian title. Owned and trained by Ann Galbraith of Waukegan, Illinois, the bitch was bred by Carol Sowders (Ch. Ketka's Beaver Woodchip x Ch. Ketka's Sure as Shootin') and completed her title in 1985. The first was *Pete* who was under Indefinite Listing Privilege.

Kimi (Kilravock Chimera) diving and catching fish. Photo courtesy of AWTA Down to Earth.

Bouncer (Ch. Madcap Bounc 'N Merrily) imitating an otter, 1990. Photo by D. Mionske.

Nancy Hughes and Ch. Chief of Lothian, UDT, CG at the starting flag.

Aside from its sporting abilities, the Border Terrier has demonstrated its delightful temperament in many ways. Several have been used as therapy dogs. These animals, after very careful screening for gentleness, friendliness and general good behavior (almost all have various obedience degrees), visit nursing homes and retirement communities. Some, such as the late Gizela Szilagyi's *Blue Jeans* (Am. and Can. Ch. Bandersnatch JubJub Bird, CDX, CG, Can. CG, bred by M. Pough), have been Certified Therapy Dogs. Blue Jeans was also the first Border to participate in the new sport of carting. Many other Borders are therapy workers, although not necessarily holding certificates from various organizations.

Another example of a very talented dog was Janice Leventhal's **Ch. Malbrant Medina CDX**, known as *Charity*, who died recently at the age of 15. She and her daughter and companion, **Ch. Faith CDX**, visited hospitals and nursing homes. Faith is now retired, but **Ch. George CD**, Charity's son, continues the tradition — also visiting homes for disturbed and homeless children. Mrs. Leventhal's dogs have made television

Three Borders and friends at the Northeast Scottish Games. Photo courtesy of N. Hiscock.

Ch. Lothlorien's Easy Strider, UD, WC, CG.

Hurdle racing. Photo courtesy of J. and G. Amidon.

Kimi earning her Herding Instinct Certificate, 1989. Photo courtesy of BTCA
Borderlines.

Ch. Faith, CDX and scent hurdles, 1985.

Ch. Hollybridge Raffles, UDT, CG, 1991.

G. Szilagyi's Blue Jeans (Ch. Bandersnatch Jubjub Bird, CDX, CG) with her cart.

appearances and have been featured in various advertisements. Borders have appeared both on stage and in films. One such star is **Ch. Sandy MacGregor Von Hasselwick** (Farmway Sandling x Clarfar Tawny of Rema, bred by F. Mettler), owned by Hazel and Jennifer Wichman of New Jersey. Sandy began her career in a Little Theater production of *Annie*. She also portrayed Dorothy's dog Toto in a school production of *The Wizard of Oz*. In 1988, Sandy appeared as the family dog in the movie *Running on Empty*. Not content with these achievements, this versatile Border is a registered Therapy Dog, has a CD degree and a CG. Born in 1976, Sandy is still going strong.

The relatively new sport of flyball is one that is much enjoyed by Borders. In this activity, the dog runs at full speed over hurdles to a box with a lever. When the lever is hit by the dog, a ball pops out from the box by a spring mechanism. The contestant catches the ball, races back over the hurdles, and returns his catch to the owner. This exciting game is also played as a relay race, with teams competing for prizes. Somewhat similar is scent hurdling, in which the dog is required to select a specific object and return to the owner, again over low hurdles both ways, in a race against time. This is really a refinement of advanced obedience work.

Borders will also play Frisbee. In fact, Karen Pryor has written *How to Teach Your Dog to Play Frisbee* (published by Simon and Schuster, 1985), which features her Border **Skookum** in photographs illustrating the sport. "Skookum," writes Mrs. Pryor, "is a Northwest Indian word meaning sturdy or very strong but not necessarily beautiful."

Ch. Sandy MacGregor V. Hasselwick, CD in a Little Theater production of Annie.

Obedience champion Ketka's Fine O'Pinyon, CG.

Perhaps the only field in which Borders do not excel is that of guarding and protecting. They will protect poultry, however, as Border owner Arthur Yanoff proved. His young **Albert** went to ground at the tender age of six weeks. Although he hunted woodchucks and other pests, he was reliable with poultry. He and his hunting companion, a Miniature Bull Terrier, were trained to drive strange dogs off their property. Albert also gave tongue when strangers appeared. So your Border companion, although friendly, will notify you of any unfamiliar visitors.

Sadly, at least one brave little Border gave her life to defend her owner. Patricia Quinn of Alabama had a much loved **Tuppy** (Am and Can. Ch. Avim Dainty Girl, CG WC) who saved her from being bitten by a water moccasin that had found its way into the Quinns' barn. Tuppy dashed between Mrs. Quinn and the snake, tackled and killed it, but was fatally bitten in the process.

"Charity" visiting a friend in a nursing home.

Flyball with Ch. Faith, CDX.

Skookum learning to play with the Frisbee.

Kimi and Bouncer on Agility A-frame.

Luvemur's Hail 'N' Hardy, CD, AD over the hurdles, 1991. Photo by C. Dostal.

Disaster dog training for Kimi and Bouncer through the North American Search Dog Network, 1990.

Agility is another relatively new activity that is rapidly gaining adherents. The dog, working against the clock, runs a complicated course. Among the obstacles are tunnels, a teeter-totter, and an A-frame. Accompanied by the owner, the dog goes full tilt, except for a brief stay command. This sport makes for top condition for both Border and owner.

One of the more unusual activities this versatile breed has tackled is herding. In 1989, *Kimi*, officially **Kilravock Chimera** (Trails End Tradesman x Todfield Tadpole, bred by D. Kline), earned her American Herding Breeds Association (AHBA) Herding Instinct Certificate by working sheep. The following year, she won a second, but the AHBA no longer grants awards to non-herding breeds, so it's not official. Owned and trained by Debra Mionske of Mt. Prospect, Illinois, Kimi holds an impressive list of titles: CD, from both AKC and UKC (United Kennel Club); a CDX from the UKC; CG, HC, TT, HIC, HTC, TDI and Canine Good Citizen. Now seven years old, she's entering Agility. In addition, she has worked in search and rescue.

Bouncer, or **Ch. Madcap Bounc'N Merrilly** (Ch. Ketkas Im A Madcap Harrier CG FDCH x Ch. Madcap's Widget of Rohan UD, WC, CG, FDX), is the second of Ms. Mionske's Borders. Just over two years old, she holds CG, HC, TT, OGC, USDAA Agility Dog titles and is a Therapy Dog International. She is starting in tracking and plays flyball.

A Border that merits more than a brief reference is Sally and Ted Nists' *Shannon.* This Irish and American champion is formally **Ch. Rossturc Oonagh CD**. She is also known as the "Diplomat Dog." The Nists acquired her in Ireland when Mr. Nist was posted there with the State Department. They took Shannon to Ulan Bator, Mongolia, by way of Russia in 1989. For the harsh winter cold, at times far below minus 20 zero, she was decked out in a hooded down suit, specially tailored, in addition to leather and knit leggings.

This Border Terrier was a great hit with the people of Mongolia, especially the children, to whom a pet dog was a great novelty. Dogs in Mongolia are usually strictly utilitarian, being used for herding or guarding.

Mrs. Nist reports that Shannon's fame was wide-spread, and this canine good-will ambassador has appeared on a Mongolian postage stamp. It might be noted that the Nists were part of the first American diplomatic group to go to Mongolia, and Shannon did her share in cementing relations.

"Shannon" all bundled up for a walk in Mongolia, 1990.

CHAPTER 13

The Working Border Terrier

BY BARBARA KEMP

"The Border Terrier is a working terrier" is the first statement in both the British and American Standards for the breed. For the average Border Terrier owner in the U.S., the best opportunity to catch a glimpse of what this means is at a Terrier trial. Terrier trials are given by various organizations across the country, often as fundraisers for worthy causes. In areas where they are popular, they can be attended almost weekly during the season with a bit of traveling. They offer a fun day outside for you and your Border. No experience is necessary. Most Borders decide immediately that this is their idea of a good time. Put on your country clothes, check the prize list to see if you need to pack a lunch, and outfit your Border with a sturdy collar and a strong leash; for when the excitement mounts, your docile pet will probably pull for all he's worth to get nearer the action.

The day's events usually include conformation, which is more relaxed and casual than in the AKC ring. Here all varieties of Terriers, sorted by sex, age and possibly size, are judged against one another using the Standard for a working Terrier. The working Terrier Standard stresses a proper scissors bite, a strong jaw, a chest that can be spanned by a man's hand behind the shoulders, a good, hard coat, and good conditioning — lean and well muscled. The Border Terrier Standard addresses these points also, so Borders usually do well in Terrier trial conformation.

Another event is Terrier racing, which is enormously exciting and noisy. The entry is divided by sex and age (and sometimes by size) and raced on the flat over miniature hurdles, often designed to look like horse jumps. The Terriers chase a lure, which is usually fur. This can be anything from an entire fox pelt to a piece of Aunt Ethel's old mink coat. Foxtails and squirrel tails are popular lures.

The Terriers are loaded into a starting box with individual compartments and released all at one time. They follow the lure down the race course and through a nine-inch hole left in a pile of hay bales at the end. The Terriers are caught as they come through the hole and are placed in that order. There is a catcher for each Terrier raced in that event. The trick is to catch each assigned Terrier and hold him high and away from other Terriers. A Terrier frustrated in his attempt to catch the lure may accidentally clamp onto the first bit of fur in his reach! The contestants and the canine spectators bark furiously. The crowd cheers on their favorites. The din is unbelievable, but lasts only the few seconds the race is being run. Everyone laughs at the antics of the Terriers who seem to be having the time of their lives.

The atmosphere during the Go-To-Ground event is different, for this is serious business to a working Terrier. The Go-To-Ground is a simulated working situation. It gives Terrier owners a safe, structured way to demonstrate a Terrier's gameness, or willingness to work. It usually carries more points than the other events, sometimes double points. Often a Terrier cannot be eligible for the day's championship honors unless he has been entered in the Go-To-Ground. In case of a tie, the decision usually is given to the Terrier with the highest ranking in the Go-To-Ground. It is in this event that the Border Terrier owner can have the opportunity to understand his Border's heritage and purpose, and for the Border himself, the chance to remember and demonstrate it.

In 1576, Dr. Caius described the Terrier in his book, *A Treatisse of English Dogges*: "Another sorte there is which hunteth the Fox and the Badger or Greye onely, whom we call Terrars, because they . . . . creep into the ground, and by that means make afrayde, nippe, and bite the Fox and Badger . . ."

For purposes of the Terrier trial, *the earth* is constructed of wood and buried in the ground. The earth is scented with the odor of the quarry. There are usually several turns to be navigated in the dark, and sometimes dead ends to test the Terrier's skills in using his nose. The Terrier creeps along, following the scent until he reaches the quarry, usually laboratory rats, caged and protected by bars. Seeing or smelling

Ch. Lothlorien Orc Pursuit, CD, CG.

Ch. Lothlorien's Easy Strider, UD, WC, CG.

the quarry's presence, the Terrier does his best to get at the rats by digging, barking, whining, chewing and lunging at the bars. Borders are wont to use their front paws much as a cat does, snaking them through the bars to get at the animal. After a set period of working, usually a minute or less, the earth is opened and the Terrier removed, usually against his will. Most Borders consider this a marvelous game and go to it enthusiastically whenever they are invited to do so. Others may decide there must be a better method, turn and leave the earth, hoping to attack the rats from above ground. This is a sensible but disqualifying decision.

Borders accustomed to working in a natural setting on rats in the barn, woodchucks in the pasture, or perhaps even foxes in the hen houses, often refuse to work in the artificial situation after a few tries. Others, eternal optimists, are sure that this time they will get those rats and never lose a chance to try. Once released, they will fly into the earth repeatedly. Once the Border learns the game and realizes that the artificial earth is a safe situation, he zips along the tunnel at full speed bent on getting to the quarry as fast as he can. As placings are determined by time, it is the successful ones who go home with the ribbons. But it may be the Borders who come out to seek another way to the rats who, in time and with opportunity, will become the working Borders they were bred to be.

The American Working Terrier Association (AWTA) was founded in 1971 by Patricia Adams Lent for the express purpose of encouraging Terriers, owners, and breeders to understand the working Terriers heritage. Pat Lent, author of *Sport With Terriers*, which is a marvelous introduction to natural hunting, had used a variety of Terriers in various kinds of hunting. In the process, she became aware that Terriers were forgetting why they had been bred and that owners and breeders no longer understood the reasons for certain points of the breed Standards.

She began by offering an award called a Certificate of Gameness (CG) for Terriers successfully completing a Go-To-Ground event. The AWTA continues to sponsor this working trial, which consists only of a Go-To-Ground event, either alone or in conjunction with racing and conformation, organized by the sponsoring group. More than 40 AWTA trials are held now each year across the U.S.

A successful completion of the 30-foot Open Earth event earns the Terrier a Certificate of Gameness. All Terriers in the AKC Terrier group, as well as Jack Russells, Patterdales, Dachshunds and German Hunting Terriers (Jagdhund), are eligible for this award. The owner need not be a member of AWTA. The CG is recognized by the Jack Russell Club of America for its competitions. A growing number of AKC breeds accept the CG as one possible component toward the coveted Versatility Award.

Border Terriers have earned more CGs than any other AKC Terrier breed, and are second only to Jack Russell Terriers (which are not AKC listed) in numbers earned.

Currently the AKC is considering approval of a Hunting Title for Terriers, using a format similar to the AWTA Go-To-Ground. As this is written, pilot events are being sponsored across the U.S. to determine the interest among AKC breeds eligible for this sport.

Do not expect to drive up to an AWTA trial the very first time with an unworked Border and come home with a CG. Borders are notorious for being *slow to enter*. This means they take their time before deciding to work. This may take several years, especially in the slow maturing lines. They seem to know when they are finally mature enough and understand the problem well enough to go at it. The only thing one can do to hasten the process is to provide the opportunity to learn. Even then, the Border will make the decision for himself.

An AWTA trial usually offers a training period following the event. Some people keep rats to educate their Terriers to the sport, not only for Terrier trial competition, but also as an introduction to natural hunting. For despite the great interest in the Certificate of Gameness competition, the AWTA focus is on natural hunting, the CG being the introduction to this sport. In *Down To Earth*, a quarterly magazine devoted to working Terriers published by AWTA, novices and experienced Terrier people swap stories and advice. The magazine also lists the AWTA trial scheduled for that year. *Down to Earth* is sent to all members of the AWTA as part of their membership. AWTA members may earn Working and Hunting Certificates, which testify to their Terriers' work in the field.

A Working Certificate (WC) is given to a Terrier who successfully works underground, holding his quarry, giving tongue for three minutes, or bolting it. There must be evidence that the Terrier worked directly up to the quarry, but need not necessarily engaged it. Another AWTA member must witness the work.

Ch. Trails End Whiskey River, CD, CG being pulled from the artificial earth at the 1984 Racine,Wisconsin, Terrier Trial.

Tuppence (Ch. Avim Dainty Girl, WC, CG) and Piper (Eignwye Red Roses) with four of 30 rats they killed in one day.

Where is it? Blue Jeans going to ground. Photo courtesy of G. Szilagyi.

Steephollow puppies, 1988. Photo by Nancy Harrington.

The end of the hunt. Fifteen-year old Lurcher waiting to dispatch woodchuck as it is drawn by Borders. Photo by Chris and Pam Dyer.

Ready to go! L-R: Can. Ch. Lothlorien Peregrin Took, TT, CG, Am. and Can. CD; Am. and Can. Ch. Jansim Lothlorien Pepper, WC, CG, Am. and Can. CD; working Dachshund, 1990.

Ch. Otterby A Klever Kelsey, CG at work, 1990.

A Hunting Certificate (HC) is offered for a full year's work in the field, usually above ground. The Terrier must be taken out for the purpose of work and not just out for walks. The HC has been given principally for rodent or varmint control on farms, but has also been given for retrieving birds, trailing deer that have been shot and wounded, and for above-ground woodchuck hunting. It is a way for a Terrier too large to go-to-ground to be recognized. It is also for Terriers who live in areas where there is no appropriate quarry that uses underground earths as dens.

The Border Terrier is well prepared by conformation and heritage to earn these awards. His strong jaw, his fairly deep-set eyes protected from dirt and sand by adequate face furnishings, his strong neck and his tough hide make him a formidable foe. His narrow and flexible body and loose hide make it possible for him to get into tight earths. His weather-resistant coat, good feet and stamina keep him ready for action all day long. His good sense and patience keep him out of trouble with other Terriers and steady to the task. It is no wonder that this sturdy little Terrier is still worked regularly in the areas where it was bred. The Border Terrier may be the only AKC Terrier able to make that claim.

A hunt Terrier's job is to enter the hole in which the fox has been driven to ground by the hounds and bolt it, or hold it at bay until it can be dug out by the Terrier handler. The Border Terrier with his background as the shepherd's and farmer's working Terrier is quite capable and often too willing to kill the fox underground by himself. The Border then is not the Terrier of choice for traditional fox hunting, in which there are few foxes who need to be preserved.

The Border's cautious approach to work can be exasperating to the novice hunter who sees other working Terrier breeds, notably Patterdales and Jack Russells, perhaps still puppies, hard at work while his Border watches. Nevertheless, if patient, the Border owner will see the development, albeit slowly, of a steady, thorough, working Terrier — careful, but not easily put off his quarry. The Border takes his time to learn.

Perhaps even more than other Terriers, the Border should be started on small rodents. Field mice are excellent quarries for the novice Border and owner and working them successfully is harder than one might think. With permission of a landowner, take your Border to a soybean or cornfield after the harvest and point out a likely hole to him and encourage him to dig. You may need to keep him on lead until he learns to stay with you. After he digs to his first mouse or to nesting material, he is on his way. At first, he will still dig any hole you point out. As he grows clever in using his nose, he will ignore holes with nothing in them. Later, he will be able to distinguish holes with live quarry from those that contain only nesting material. It takes two Terriers digging to a central point to catch field mice on a regular basis. What a thrill when your team figures this out.

As one hunts one can teach the Border simple working commands. "Come," "leave it," "stay" and "out" (of the hole) are very helpful, and the dog should learn to return to the whistle or command. Because he should work without a collar, a simple noose-type lead that goes on and off in a jiffy is useful in the field.

Before tackling woodchuck, it is helpful to locate an experienced working Terrier person and ask to go along on a dig. Most working Terrier people are glad to introduce a seriously interested person to the sport. It is worth traveling a good distance for the opportunity. There is a great deal to learn about earth work with Terriers and the Terrier depends on his handler to protect him. One needs to know how to choose safe terrain, safe ways to dig out a Terrier, how to dispatch quarry and what to do about injuries and wounds. Earth work can be dangerous. One also needs to understand the risks involved and know what precautions to take. Most working Terrier enthusiasts use a locator collar that beeps to locate the Terrier underground — a great safety factor. It is very exciting and strenuous work for both the Terrier and owner, so both need to be in hard, working condition. If the Border has done his preliminary work on mice and rats, he will understand very quickly what is required, especially with more experienced Terriers present and working, and the owner will be rewarded by the experience of seeing the dog's heritage and skills in action.

Ch. Otterby A Trailblazer demonstrating above-ground tunnel work.

Kimi and Bouncer hunting muskrat, 1991.

Kimi and Bouncer now hunting mice, 1990.

Yadkin Valley Hounds Terrier Trails, Cleveland, North Carolina. The 25-yard dash won by the Border on the left. Photo courtesy of C. and B. Hall.

Some people feel that if a Border is worked, it will spoil him for other things. Not so. A Border that has an opportunity to understand his instincts and use them appropriately is usually steadier in other situations. Your Border who has worked all day will be just as pleased to jump up on your sofa or onto your bed that evening as ever before. There are many Borders with championships, obedience degrees, certificates of gameness and working titles, which testifies to their versatility and flexibility. Natural hunting is not everyone's sport, but it is important for a Border owner to understand its significance in the Border's heritage and to remember it in judging his conformation and in breeding programs. And for those who do know the joy of working with their Border in fields, brush piles, and barns, there is only one thing to say: "Happy hunting!"

NOTES:

The first Border Terrier to earn a Certificate of Gameness: *CH. Bandersnatch Snark, CD, CG*, owned by Margaret Pough, June 17, 1972.

The first Border Terrier to earn a Working Certificate: *Am, Can, Bda, CH. Avim Dainty Girl, CG, WC, HC*, owned by Patricia Quinn, May 7, 1977.

The first Border Terrier to earn a Hunting Certificate: *Am, Can,, Bda, CH. Avim Dainty Girl, CG, WC, HC*, owned by Patricia Quinn, June 20, 1980.

The most titled working Border to date: *CH. Trail's End Peaceful Bree, UD, CG, WC, HC, Gold ROM*, owned by JoAnn Frier-Murza.

For American Working Terrier rules see Appendix F.

CHAPTER 14

The Border Terrier in Obedience and Agility

OBEDIENCE, BY LAURALE STERN

In the past five to ten years, training Border Terriers for AKC obedience competition has increased in popularity. AKC obedience competition includes three levels of difficulty, the first being *Novice*, with such exercises as heeling on and off lead, a stand for examination, and a recall from 35 feet. The next level is *Open*, which includes heeling off lead only, a drop halfway in from the recall, two retrieves (one on the flat and the other over a high jump), and the broad jump. Both Novice and Open include a long, group Sit and Down: Novice with the handlers in sight, and Open with them out of sight. The *Utility* level is the most difficult, with exercises including signal heeling, retrieving the owner's scented article from among 10 others, marking and retrieving one of three designated gloves, going out between two jumps, sitting upon command, taking the jump indicated by the handler, and returning to a straight front. The Novice title is the CD (Companion Dog), Open is the CDX (Companion Dog Excellent) and the Utility is the UD (Utility Dog). A perfect score is 200. A dog must earn at least 170 or half of each exercise in three trials under three different judges to earn one of these titles.

Although obedience competition is primarily aimed at the sporting breeds, the Border Terrier seems well suited to take on this challenge. Since 1953, when **Philabeg Duchess**, owned by Mrs. Anthony C. Cerasale of Washington, D.C., earned the first CD in the breed, there have been 240 CDs, 71 CDXs and 27 UDs earned by Border Terriers at AKC obedience trials.

Although exercises such as retrieving, marking and taking direction at a distance are quite natural for the sporting breeds bred to hunt and retrieve birds unharmed, often from a great distance, they are completely against the instincts of a Terrier. It must be kept in mind that Terriers were bred to work independently; chasing badgers, fox and other vermin, going to ground after them, bolting them out or, if necessary, killing them. Their primary job was to rid the farmer of these predators to protect livestock and poultry in particular.

The majority of exhibitors showing Border Terriers in obedience trials didn't choose the breed primarily with AKC obedience competition in mind. Rather, they adopted the Border as a family pet or to breed and show in conformation, secondarily deciding to try their hands at training a Border for obedience exhibition. Finding obedience to be exciting and fun and willing to take on the challenge, many of these people continue past their initial Novice title and go on to the upper levels.

Obedience competition has become tougher with the introduction, in 1980, of the OTCh or Obedience Trial Championship. To earn an OTCh, the dog must have its UD, compete in both Open and Utility and place first or second, earning points according to the number of dogs competing. A total of 100 points and three first places (one from Open, one from Utility and the third from either) are required to complete this title, which precedes the dog's registered name, compared to the other titles which follow the name. This prestigious title has been earned by only two Border Terriers in the history of the breed: *OTCh Pete, UD*, owned by Floyd E. Timmons of Detroit, Michigan (1978) and *OTCh Ketkas Fine O'Pinyon, UD*, owned by Anne Galbraith of Waukegan, Illinois (1985). With the OTCh has come an increased number of professional trainers. These professionals not only seek out the perfect dog for this type of intense competition, but continue to develop better training methods to achieve near-perfect performances. Scores of 197 and 198 are often needed even to place in these competitive levels. Once again, the Border Terrier can achieve these levels with hard work and perseverance on the part of his handler, but, because these exercises are totally foreign to the Border, consistently strong performances are difficult to attain and non-qualifications are not uncommon. A good sense of humor is needed when your Border Terrier drops on his belly to catch a fly on the Long Sit, retrieves the glove but refuses to release it until it is *killed*, or continues straight out of the ring on the final about turn in the heeling pattern.

Despite all of this, in the past two to three years, scores of 195-198 were seen more frequently throughout the country and at all levels by Border Terriers and their handlers. But, more importantly, more Borders are being seen in the obedience rings at AKC obedience events than ever before. Certainly much of this is due to BTCA encouraging its members to compete in obedience and acknowledging their accomplishments. Not only are certificates awarded to handlers whose dogs earned AKC obedience titles, but their names and titles are announced at the annual meeting following the National Specialty. This is truly a rarity among national breed clubs. Obedience competition is offered at all specialty shows and the dog with the highest qualifying score is awarded the Chief of Lothlan Award, named after the first UD Border Terrier, **Ch. Chief of Lothian, UDT**, owned and trained by Nancy Hughes of West Chicago, Illinois (1973). Chief was the first Border Terrier to earn a bench championship, a Utility Degree and a Tracking title.

Training a Border Terrier to compete in obedience is both challenging and rewarding. Those of us who have taken on this challenge have no regrets and agree that the Border Terrier is indeed deserving of its reputation as a versatile Terrier able to do it all!

AGILITY, BY CAROLYN DOSTAL

Border Terriers are very trainable for Agility and really seem to love it. In observing my own two Borders in class and comparing them to the other breeds, I would say that because of the Borders' outgoing, fearless nature they seem to have less difficulty than other breeds in the more difficult obstacles. Agility does build confidence and requires no heavy-hand corrections, so even the shy Border would have no problem learning the obstacles and competing.

The drawback that I have found in training the Border is gaining control off-lead and having the dog working away from the handler. I have one Border that has excellent control off-lead but hates to work away from me. This means a lot of running for me (great exercise). My other Border will work away from me, but I don't always feel that I have control.

Because Agility trials are held mostly outside, control is very necessary and I do recommend being very careful before trusting your Border off-lead.

The United States Dog Agility Association, Inc. (USDAA) was founded in 1986 for the promotion of uniform international standards for dog agility. Membership is permitted by both local agility clubs and individual members, and dogs are able to compete without regard to pedigree. Jump and obstacle heights and distances are based on dogs height at the withers.

Agility certification titles include:

> *Agility Dog.* The dog must achieve a clear round (no faults) in the Starters or Novice Class pursuant to the rules and regulations of the USDAA.
> *Advanced Agility Dog.* The dog must achieve three clear rounds under two different judges.
> *Master Agility Dog.* This is a four-part qualification process. Dog must achieve a clear round in the Masters class. Cumulatively, this will mean that the dog has been tested through three levels (Starters or Novice, Advanced and Masters) achieving flawless performances a minimum of five times under three different judges. In addition, the dog must have received qualifying scores in each of the following non-regular classes:
> 1. Gamblers Competition
> 2. Team, Pairs Relay or Team Relay
> 3. A third non-standard class. A dog may not qualify twice in a class under the same judge.

To date, there is one Master Agility Dog.

CHAPTER 15

The Border Terrier Around the World

AUSTRIA, BY ING. KURT RADNETTER

The first Border Terrier litters in Austria were born in the 1950s, but no information is available on them. In 1963, a litter bred by Fürstin Hohenlohe was registered in the Austrian studbook. In 1985, Mrs. Margarete Huber, whose kennel name is *vom Lärchenbruch,* imported the bitch **Rocheby Skippalong** from England (Savinroyd President x Skippers Girl). Among her many titles was that of World Champion in 1990. She is a very "typey" bitch, and most Austrian lines are based on her. Having been shown extensively, she has done much for the popularity of Borders in Austria.

Other imports have come from England, Denmark and Germany. In their pedigrees are seen such well-known names as Oxcroft President, Brumberhill Blue Maestro, Duttonlea Suntan of Dandyhow and Mansergh Pearldiver.

Currently there are five breeders, and about 40 to 50 puppies are registered each year.

Breeders at present are:

vom Lärchenbruch - Margarete Huber
vom Jagerhansl - Johann Nechwatal
von der Birkenheide - Josef Hridlicka
Sky Yards - Annelies Reisinger
Otterburn - M. L. Doppelreiter/ P. Wieser

This information was kindly sent by Ing. Kurt Radnetter of Vienna, president of the Austrian Terrier Club.

An Austrian Border Terrier.

VSP   KELGRAM THE MINSTREL

From the Finnish **Border Terrier News,** *1991.*

FINLAND, BY LEENA HARJAPÄÄ

The pioneer of the breed in Finland is Miss Brita Donner, and her *Monkans* Borders have been known since the early 1950s. The British breed Standard is followed in Finland, because Finland is a member of the FCI, where all the Standards are based on the original country of the breed.

Miss Donner, after moving back to Finland in 1950 from Sweden, brought **Mellby Monkey,** the first Border Terrier ever in Finland. It is interesting to find that many Finnish and Swedish Border breeders have based their breeding on the Monkans lines.

The Finnish Border Terrier breeders have cooperated with the Swedish breeders, and Sweden has given a lot to our Border Terrier breeding. Unfortunately, for the past few years it has been impossible to cooperate very much because Sweden closed its borders because there were some rabies' cases in Finland.

There is one dog whose name must be mentioned when speaking about the Finnish Border Terriers. He is Nordic Winner (1980, 1981, 1983) and Finnish Winner (1980-1987, 1991) *Int & Nord Ch. Farmway Southern Hawk*, who was sent to Finland from the United Kingdom (UK) by Mrs. Madeline Aspinwall. This dog really opened the eyes of the Finnish people to the Border Terriers because he always showed like a bomb and showed that Border Terriers can also win the groups, even the great finals. He really has been the star, and he has left some nice progeny. Among them, the best one might be his daughter, *Rabalder Milda Makter*, who was the Youth World Winner in Copenhagen in 1989 under Mr. C. G. Stafberg from Sweden and Finnish Winner in 1991. Her dam is *Int & Finnish & Swedish Ch. Tallarnas Latoss Gissa* and her breeder is the famous Swedish breeder Mrs. A. K. Bergh. She came to Finland as a pick of litter.

Milda Makter has had one litter by Finnish dual Champion, Finnish Winner 1989, and World Winner 1990 *Int Ch. Brackenhills Flagman*, whose sire is the son of *Ch. Brannigan of Brumberhill*. In this litter were two brothers who have been very successful in the shows: *Kletters Mac William*, who was made European winner by Mr. Ronald Irving in 1991, and *Kletters Mac Kenzie*, who has also had success in hunting trials. The *Kletters* prefix is owned by Mrs. Aune Luoso who has always had an eye for good Borders because all the above mentioned Borders in Finland belong to her, or she has bred them. We have imported some very interesting Borders recently from England together with many imports from Sweden. Worthy of mentioning must be the three *Kelgram* Borders bred by Mr. and Mrs. Sam Mitchell in the UK. First, in 1966, they sent the grizzle bitch *Ch. Kelgram This's Mist at Ulaani*, by Dandyhow Mardil at Kelgram x Brehill March Secret at Kelgram. Unfortunately, Mist never produced any litters, although she was mated to the Swedish import *Ch. Bombax Nelson* who was BOB under Mrs. Peggy Grayson at the Specialty. The sister of Mist in the UK was mated to *Ch. Bushnells Turtle*, and she had a litter from which Mr. and Mrs. Mitchell sent to Finland the grizzle bitch *Kelgram My Love*, who has seldom been shown but who always placed. *Kelgram The Minstrel* by Dandyhow Mardil at Ulaani x Dusky Ice

Maiden at Kelgram came to Finland two years ago and has been very successful in shows and has already sired litters. He has been also very promising in the artificial fox hunting trial, but he is so young that he has plenty of time to show what he really is.

Mrs. Tuija Saari has imported bitches from Sweden and from Mr. Robson from Digbrack in the UK. She has a promising young bitch, *Digbrack Candy Tuft*, as well as *Ch. Ljungeldens Second Hand News*, who was mated one year ago in Germany to *Int & GB & D Ch. & A Ch. Digbrack Barley Sugar. Second Hand News* is the Swedish-bred one.

The Finnish Border Terrier people have been very active in the shows. Our winters don't allow opportunities to use the Borders for hunting because we usually have a lot of snow and the temperature might be -20° C or lower, but in the springtime and autumn we have many artificial underground tests for the Borders and breeds like Fox Terriers, German Hunting Terriers and Dachshunds. We have some dual champions in our breed, and we try always to remember that the Border Terrier is a hunting breed with all the breed characteristic features.

The Finnish Border Terrier Club arranges many activities for its members. Every year, we have a club show, which in 1991 had 80 Borders entered under Mrs. Kirsti Smith, who was the judge. The Fox Day in April has also been very popular. During the day, the members have the chance to watch the artificial underground tests, and if they are interested there is always the opportunity to try their own dogs. It is not so difficult because most of Borders, if they are not too young, are very eager to go to the tunnel after the fox. They really enjoy being in the tunnel and barking at the fox. It is their life!

In Finland, we register about 70 puppies per year. We try to have special judges in our Specialties and also for the biggest shows arranged by the Finnish Kennel Club.

Today, the breed is very popular in our country, and it is our task to keep the Border sound in construction and also in temperament.

GREAT BRITAIN, 1981-1991, BY ROBERT AND RUTH ANN NAUN

To do a complete survey of the Border Terrier in Great Britain in such a short space would be impossible. There has been a tremendous increase in the last decade in the number of new Border Terrier breeders, kennels and exhibitors in the show ring. Evidence of this is the growth in size of membership in the Border Terrier Club from approximately 420 members to more than 700 between 1981 and 1991; entries in championship shows have almost doubled and there has been a doubling of the number of Border Terrier clubs. The Scottish, Northern and Midland clubs started during this period, with the proposal of at least one other club in the near future. It is our intention to discuss the winning kennels during the past decade and the contribution in the United States of these kennels to the development of the Border Terrier during the 1980s.

In surveying the lists of Challenge Certificate (CCs) winners and Reserve Challenge Certificate (RCCs) winners over the decade, the names of a number of kennels repeatedly appear, several of which produced a number of champions for other kennels.

Of the long active and established kennels, we find the *Dandyhow* kennel of Mrs. Bertha Sullivan and Mrs. Kate Irving, the *Clipstone* kennel of Jean and Frank Jackson, the *Farmway* prefix of Madeline Aspinwall, the *Mansergh* prefix of Anne Roslin Williams, and the *Duttonlea* kennel of Wilf Wrigley. Of the relatively new kennels, we see the *Thoraldby* prefix of Peter and Maureen Thompson, the *Brumberhill* prefix of Stewart McPherson, and a number of smaller kennels winning in the show ring.

The *Dandyhow* kennel dates back to the early 1950s. In the past decade, it has finished six champions including **Ch. Duttonlea Suntan of Dandyhow, Ch. Dandyhow Scotsman, Ch. Uncle Walter of Dandyhow, Ch. Dandyhow Crofter** and **Ch. Valmyre Magician of Dandyhow.**

In 1982, **Ch. Dandyhow Scotsman** achieved Reserve Best Terrier at Crufts and the latest Dandyhow champion, **Ch. Valmyre Magician of Dandyhow,** won Best of Breed at Crufts. The Dandyhow stud force, at our last counting, sired more than 12 champions for other kennels in the period from 1981 to 1991. The influence of Dandyhow has also been present in the United States. It has been primarily the stud services of **Am. Ch. Dandyhow Brass Tacks**, an American ROM winner, who accompanied his owners/breeders, Ronnie and Kate Irving, when they spent several years in the US on business. Brass Tacks has since returned with the family to Britain leaving five American champion get. Brass Tacks was sired by *Dandyhow April Fool,* who also sired *Am. Ch. Hollybridge Red Jester. Ch. Dandyhow Crofter* sired the *Am. Ch. Dandyhow Top Notch.* Both *Am. Ch. Hollybridge Red Jester* and *Am. Ch. Dandyhow Top Notch* have produced champion progeny in the US.

The *Clipstone* prefix of the Jacksons has either bred or finished seven champions in the last decade. They are *Ch. Clipstone Comma, Ch. Clipstone Cumin, Ch. Clipstone Chasse, Ch. Tearose of Stonekite, Ch. Clipstone Slapdash, Ch. Stonekite Charisma by Clipstone,* and *Ch. Stonekite Soap by Clipstone* as their latest champion. The Clipstone stud force sired several champions for other kennels, including *Ch. Ragsdale Whynot, Ch. Bannerdown Boomerrang* and *Ch. Bannerdown Cavalier.* The Clipstone influence in the US has been limited in the past decade although several American kennels, Oldstone, Cymri Hill and Highdyke can trace many of their pedigrees back to *Clipstone Cider Rose* and *Am. Ch. Borderseal Bessie,* both sired by *Ch. Clipstone Guardsman,* and both of whom were imported in the early 1970s.

The *Thoraldby* kennel of Peter and Maureen Thompson has produced or finished seven champions in the last decade, including *Ch. Thoralby Free Guest, Ch. Thoraldby Traveller, Ch. Thoraldby Glenfiddich, Ch. Loristan Amber, Ch. Thoraldby Tolomeo, Ch. Thoraldby Noble Flyer* and *Ch. Thoraldby Tiptoes.* They also campaigned *Ch. Loristan Amber* to her winning the Terrier group at the Scottish Kennel Club show in 1982. This kennel has the honor of having the only two group winning British Border bitches, the other being *Ch. Thoraldby Yorkshire Lass.* The Thompsons have been frequent visitors to the US as judges and guests, and their kennel has had an important impact there through the kennels of Barbara Kemp, Jim Kane and Pat Quinn. The most recent import from that kennel was *Br. Am. Ch. Thoraldby Free Guest* owned by Kate Seeman. We are starting to see some of his offspring in the rings today. Another Thoraldby import co-owned by Mrs. Seeman and Sam Ewing III is *Am. Ch. Thoraldby Tomahawk.*

The *Brumberhill* affix of Stewart McPherson has made a tremendous impact in the past decade. Beginning in 1982, the Brumberhill kennel has produced, or finished more than seven champions. The most outstanding Border of the past decade, *Ch. Brannigan of Brumberhill*, comes from this kennel. By *Ch. Blue Maverick of Brumberhill*, Brannigan won 31 CCs, 10 Reserve CCs, seven Groups, six Reserve Groups, four Best in Show, and three Reserve Best in Shows (including Crufts and Top Puppy 1985). He won Top Border in 1986, 1987, 1988 and BOB at Crufts in 1987, 1988 and 1989. He has sired numerous champions and continues to do so.

Other well known champions produced by this kennel were *Ch. Brumberhill Blue Maestro* who won four CCs as a puppy and a total of nine before being exported to Holland, and *Ch. Brumberhill Bittersweet* who had a Reserve in the Terrier Group. Other champions included in this kennel were *Ch. Blue Lace of Brumberhill* and *Ch. Blue Maverick of Brumberhill*. Being a rather recent name on the Border scene in Britain, the Brumberhill kennel has not as yet had a great deal of impact here in the US. There have been two dogs sired by Brannigan imported to the US who have achieved their championships: *Am. Ch. Cheltorian Mischief at Brumberhill* by Camilla Moon who sired *Am. Ch. Highdyke Lilly of Trillium*, and *Am. Ch. Plushcourt Gangster* imported by Lois and Al Langish. However, considering the impact of this kennel in Britain, we expect to see a greater influence in the next decade.

The long established kennel of Madeline Aspinwall, *Farmway*, has had success in the show ring and an impact in the US, while having a number of champions in her kennel in the last decade, including *Ch. Farmway Fine Feathers, Ch. Farmway Money Bird, Ch. Thoraldby Star, Appeal of Lardach* and *Farmway M'lady Robin*. The most influential Farmway champion was *Ch. Farmway Snow Kestrel* who sired *Ch. Lyddington Lets Go, Ch. Llanishen Red Eagle* and *Ch. Richvale Festive Gift*. His offspring exported to the US include *Am. Ch. Farmway Show Song* and the ROM winners *Am. Ch. Farmway Cherry Wren* and *Am. Ch. Farmway Sparrowhawk*.

The *Mansergh* prefix of Anne Roslin Williams and her mother has been well known in the British show ring over the past decade. They campaigned *Ch. Linne of Duthill* to eight CCs. They followed these successes with *Ch. Froswick Button of Mansergh, Ch. Mansergh Toggle, Ch. Mansergh Tassel*, and *Ch. Mansergh Denim*. While Mansergh has exported several prominent Borders to the continent, there have been few Borders sent to this country.

Another small kennel that has had success in the British show ring in the last decade, as well as having impact upon the show ring in the US is the *Duttonlea* kennel of Wilf Wrigley. Mr. Wrigley's greatest success came through the breeding of his brood bitch, **Ribbleside Morning Dew** to *Dandyhow Grenadier*. This cross produced the famous brother-sister success story in *Ch. Duttonlea Steel Blue* and *Ch. Duttonlea Suntan of Dandyhow*. *Ch. Duttonlea Steel Blue*, until being overtaken by *Ch. Nettleby Mellein*, had been the Border bitch with the highest number off CCs (11) in the breed. The litter brother of the pair, *Am. Ch. Duttonlea Autocrat of Dandyhow*, was imported into the US by Nancy Hughes. He was Best of Breed at the National Specialty in 1982, 1983 and 1986, and is the sire of 41 American champions. His impact on the breed continues through his sons, *Am. Ch. Todfield Trafalgar Square*, Gold ROM, and *Am. Ch. Trails End Buddy of Glen Farm*, Gold ROM, as well as being behind many of the American-bred National Specialty winners. The influence of the Duttonlea kennel is also seen through the offspring of *Am. Ch. Duttonlea Genie*, the mother of the 1987 National Specialty Best of Breed, *Am. Ch. Tansy of Steephollow*, and through *Am. Ch. Duttonlea Jenny Wren*, the mother of the Best of Opposite Sex winner, *Am. Ch. Red Baron of Steephollow*, at the same National Specialty.

The *Nettleby* prefix of Mr. and Mrs. Tuck has also been successful in Britain in recent years, and has had an impact on the American Border fancy. Their successful stud dog, *Ch. Lyddington Lets Go*, sired *Ch. Nettleby Mellein*, who holds the record for winning the most CCs (18) of any Border bitch in the history of the breed in Britain. *Ch. Lyddington Lets Go*'s offspring in the US include *Am. Ch. Nettleby Nighthawk*, winner of the 1990 American Specialty, and *Am. Ch. Rockferry Bomber Boy*, Winners Dog at the 1991 American Specialty.

Finally, there are two other kennels that have achieved success in Britain, and based on their initial records, deserve mention. These include the *Foxwyn* prefix of Mr. and Mrs. Hodgson whose kennel produced *Ch. Foxwyn Shoot a Line*, sire of *Ch. Lynsett Trouble Shooter*, and *Ch. Foxtor Blue Jester*, sire of the well-known stud dog, *Cheltnor Michael*. Also included would be the *Dykeside* prefix of Mr. and Mrs. Brian

Staveley who in the 1980s bred *Ch. Blue Doctor* and *Ch. Dykeside Gordon Ranger*, both of whom have had influence as stud dogs. *Ch. Dykeside Gordon Ranger* sired *Am. Ch. Dykeside Kristina*, imported by Elizabeth Crisp Blake.

The past 10 years have been active and growing ones for the Border Terrier in Great Britain. This is but a brief summary of the achievements of the successful kennels in the show ring, and where appropriate, their influence in the United States in the last decade.

L-R: German Ch. Kiki's Mistress Anna, Rina v. Tinsdal (grandaughter of Dt. and World Ch. Kiki's Mr. Moses).

GERMANY, BY CHRISTOFER F. HABIG

Compared to other European countries like Sweden, Finland and The Netherlands, the Border Terrier is still a relatively rare breed in Germany — kept and shown just by a small dedicated fraternity.

Eng. and German and World Ch. Thoraldby Glenfiddich, first group winning Border Terrier in Germany. Photo by K. V. Peisker.

What constitutes a considerable contribution to the Border's popularity in other countries, chiefly the hunting, field and agility competitions, have never been as much an integrated part of our dog scene as elsewhere. While the German hunting scene, apart from the world of the show ring, is still dominated by the well-established German Hunting Terrier, the agility field, which spotlights the Border in Sweden, has not yet really conquered German dogdom. That is to say: The back bone of German Border breeding has traditionally been a handful of enthusiasts who have built up the breed on their own merits, providing for a certain degree of exclusivity.

The Border Terrier was introduced to Germany in the mid-1950s by an American Rhine Army Captain from Washington, D.C., who was stationed near Bonn. His pair of Borders, purchased in Britain and going back to Raisgill breeding (H. Garnett-Orme), are the first representatives of the breed, and who were registered in 1956 by the *Klub fur Terrier e.V. (KfT)*, the German national breed club founded in 1894, covering 25 different Terrier breeds.

The first German-bred litters from these dogs, though, as well as from the other two imports in the '50s, were never used for further breeding, nor did they leave their mark in the show ring. The same applies to Mr. H. Wöhl's *Roemerschanze* kennel (better known for its Boston Terriers), where the fourth German Border litter was bred eight years later in August 1966, out of two imported *Tedhars* (E. Harper). Although Mr. Wöhl's Borders produced another six litters up to 1971, and found one or the other newcomer to use his dogs for a few further litters, none of these puppies grew into the role of a foundation for those breeders who were later the ones actually to build up the Border Terrier in Germany. Nevertheless, the red *Tedhars Traveller*, Mr. Wöhl's imported stud going back to *Engl. Ch. Barnikin*, is our country's first Border Terrier who gained his title as German Champion (Dt. Ch) and German Bundessieger in 1965.

This somewhat hesitant start of the German Border breeding proves what can be documented worldwide in so many other breeds, too: No breed will ever get off the ground in any country unless it has found its authentic stalwart. At best this is a gifted person of deep knowledge in dogs, of keen and long-lasting devotion to the breed, of lively contacts to the breed's home country and with a good name in the dog world.

The person who played this vital role in German Borders was Miss W. Steen from Harsefeld near Hamburg. Up to this date, she is the indefatigable *Doyen* of the breed in Germany — setting the standards in terms of concentration on type and temperament, consistency in line-breeding and care for her Border companions up to highest age. Coming from a family background in Scottish Terriers, which goes well back to pre-war times, Miss Steen registered her own Scottie kennel under the *Kiki's* prefix in 1947 (where Scotties were successfully bred for nearly 40 years), before she took the Border Terrier under her wing in 1965, when she purchased *Portholme Merrybelle* from Mrs. P. Mulcaster.

As the second lady judge for all the different Terrier breeds in the history of the German Terrier Club, awarding CCs in the UK already in the '60s, Miss Steen was the person required to give the breed the authoritative backing needed. She published feature articles on Borders, introduced the breed to the show ring and single-handedly prepared the ground for all those who joined the Border fraternity in the following years.

The first Border litter under the *Kiki's* prefix was born in September 1967, actually the seventh litter of the breed in Germany. It was by *Traveller* out of *Merrybelle* (by *Ch. Joytime* x *Ch. Portholme March Belle*). Merrybelle became the first German bitch champion and the first bitch Bundessieger title holder in 1968 — her two daughters, *Borderbeauty* and *Borderbelle*, the first German bred Border Terrier champions. The dog, though, who played the role of the breed's major ambassador in Germany was *Engl. Ch. Deerstone Dugmore*, Miss Steen's second import (born in 1966 by *Ch. Portholme Mr. Moses* x *Deerstone Judy*, bred by Mr. R. Hall), being the first English Border Terrier champion to be exported to the continent. Dugmore, who sired litters up to the age of 13, became the breed's first World Champion title holder in the history of FCI at Budapest in 1971, and also gained the titles of International, Luxembourg and Dt. Champion. Via his son, *Dt. Ch. Kiki's Mr. Moses*, FCI-World Champion at Innsbruck/Austria of 1976 and the breed's first Europe-Sieger in 1974, who came out of a father-daughter mating (his mother being *Internat. & Dt. & World Ch. Kiki's Baffle*), one of Kiki's present lines can be traced 25 years back to the kennel's foundation.

Among Kiki's major British imports up to the year 1990 are *Internat. & Dt. Ch. Bugs Billy* (son of *Ch. Dandyhow Scotsman*, bred by Mr. A. Irving), *Dt. Ch. Campanologia Snarker Pike* (son of *Ch. Thoraldby Tiptoes*, bred by Miss M. S. Churchill), *Engl. & Internat. & Austr. & Swiss & Dt. Ch. Digbrack Barley Sugar* (son of *Thoraldby Night Owl*, bred by Mr. G. Robson), *Internat. & Dt. Ch. Thoraldby Another Amber* (daughter of *Ch. Thoraldby Tiptoes* x *Ch. Loiriston Amber*, one of two group winning Border bitches to date in Britain, bred by Mr. and Mrs. P. Thompson), and finally *Engl. & Dt. Ch.*

Thoraldby Glenfiddich (son of **Ch. & US Ch. Thoraldby Free Guest**). Glenfiddich, who gained the FCI-World Champion title at Dortmund/Germany in 1991 under Mr. K. B. Staveley, made history by being the first Border Terrier to win the Terrier group at one of Germany's All Breed Championship shows in October 1991 under Swiss Terrier authority Mrs. E. Clerc.

When reviewing the 34 years of Border Terrier breeding in Germany from 1956 to 1990, there are only three other kennels besides Kiki's that have produced 10 or more litters during all these years: *Cheeky Chum's, v. Tinsdal,* and *v.d. Lochowburg.* Though differing in their principles and practices, they are the ones that are behind most of the kennels that were established in the late 1980s. In total, the German Terrier Club (KfT) has registered 672 Border Terriers up to 1990, including 60 imports.

In December 1979, Cheeky Chum's had its first litter — actually this was the 27th litter of the breed in Germany. Mr. J. Rosner, running one of Europe's leading kennels in Irish Wolfhounds (reg. 1974 under the Oelmuehle affix with Mr. J. Papenfuss), started with two imported Workmores from Mrs. E. Pope: **Dt. Ch. Headlad of Workmore**, a son of **Engl. & US Ch. Workmore Waggoner**, and **Workmore Jubilation**, double granddaughter of Waggoner. Headlad sired five litters at Cheeky Chum's up to August 1981, twice mated to one of his daughters x Jubilation. He was followed by the kennel's second study, **Internat. & Dt. Ch. Cedarcourt Nettle**, purchased from F. G. Baldwin, a son of Swedish bred **Engl. & Nord. Ch. Bombax Xavier**, imported to England by Mr. and Mrs. F. Jackson (Clipstone). Nettle sired well over 10 litters at Cheeky Chum's. The kennel's present stud is **Internat. & Dt. Ch. Plushcourt Echo**, bred by Mrs. B. A. Judge out of a Dandyhow bitch sired by **Ch. Mansergh Pearl-Diver**, who was later exported to The Netherlands, where he contributed considerably to the development of the bred.

The foundation bitch of Mrs. G. Gutschow (Hamburg) at Tinsdal (est. 1975 for WHW-Terriers) was **Chevinor Rosanna** (by **Ch. Ribbleside Ridgeman**), born in 1977 and bred by Mr. A. H. Beardwood. Rosanna, gaining the Internat. & Lux. & Dt. Ch. title, had her first litter in April 1980, by **Dt. & World Ch. Kiki's Mr. Moses**. One of the puppies, **Rachel v. Tinsdal**, went to Miss Steen and could be made up Internat. & Dt. Champion. **Chevinor Ribbon** by **Ch. Beenaben Brock** became Tinsdal's second foundation, mated to a Dugmore son, **Dt. Ch. Humpty Dumpty's Ankel** (Mr. C. Bischof) produced Tinsdal's second litter. One of the Tinsdals that was particularly influential in German Border breeding, was **Rossa v. Tinsdal**, daughter of W. Steen's **Internat. & Dt. Ch. Bugs Billy** and **Roslyn v. Tinsdal**, who was by Kiki's **Mr. Moses. Rossa**, mated to Miss Steen's **Dt. Ch. Campanologia Snarker Pike**, produced **Internat. & Danish & Dt. Ch. Don v. Vogthof** (bred by A. v. Appen), who holds the Working Certificate in Germany, Denmark and CSFR. Don belongs to those German-bred Borders that spotlight the working characteristics of the dogs who were imported by Kiki's.

The two sires that started off the *Lochowburg* kennel of Mr. W. V. Lochow from Spenge were Rosner's **Internat. & Dt. Ch. Cedarcourt Nettle**, producing Mr. Lochow's successful own stud, **Internat. & Lux. & Dt. Ch. Alf v.d. Lochowburg**, and **Engl. & Internat. & Danish & Dutch & World Ch. Duttonlea Suntan of Dandyhow** (grandson of the famous **Ch. Dandyhow Nightcap**), who had been exported to Denmark. Suntan produced **Dt. Ch. Digger v.d. Lochowburg**. Lochow's foundation bitch was **Internat. & Dt. Ch. Saredon Peggy Sue**, who on the mother's side goes back to **Ch. Napoleon Brandy**, was purchased from A. J. Bradley in the UK.

For the last years reviewed in this brief portrait, the German Border Terrier scene is considerably widening. More people got interested in the breed due to its health, natural charm and handy size. The traditionally small number of yearly imports has risen from five in 1988 to 14 in 1990, when a total of 96 Border Terriers were registered. The latest figures show the steady increase: 142 Borders registered in 1991, containing 131 puppies and 11 imports. From the 25 imports in the last two years, 16 came from the UK, three from The Netherlands, two from Denmark and Austria and one each from Sweden and Switzerland. Compared to other countries, this is just "small-scale business." Considering the total number of Borders in our country, this rapid boom will bring a considerable change of our situation. If commercialism can be avoided and the good potentials from different sources are wisely coordinated, we in Germany are looking into a bright future in Border Terriers.

Irish Ch. Rossturc Ivy.

IRELAND, BY SUSAN M. MILNE, ROSSTURC BORDER TERRIERS, COUNTY CLARE, IRELAND

In 30 years, there have only been 10 Irish champions, which really tells you a great deal about the breed in Ireland. At a good show such as the St. Patrick's Day Show, the total entry would be around 16 Border Terriers. At most shows the entry would be more like six.

For many years, there have only been two breeders, myself and Denis Murphy from Co. Meath. More recently, Mr. D. McLernan from Ballycastle in Co. Antrim has been taking a great interest and become involved in breeding.

Although I never have any difficulty selling puppies, they don't seem to get into the show ring, and I can't see the situation changing much in the next few years, in spite of the fact that in England the Border Terrier is now one of the most popular Terriers.

Irish Ch. Plushcourt Tactic at Rathvarraig, 1991.

1964	Mrs. P. Bennett	*DANDYHOW BECKY SHARP OF ARDCAIRN*
		Br. Mrs. B. Sullivan
		Fighting Fettle/Beautiful Spy
1967	Mrs. P. Bennett	*ARDCAIRN ROWAN*
		Br. Mrs. P. Bennett
		Dandyhow Shillelagh/Sweet Sue of Ardcairn
1976	Mr. D. P. Murphy	*RATHVARRAIG COR-ABBEY GULL*
		Br. Mr. M. Barry
		Hawkesburn John/Farmway Barley Gull
1977	Mr. D. P. Murphy	*ALAMOSA NEON*
		Br. Mrs. E. A. Cleveland
		Farmway Diver/Huntcombe Tarka of Tor
1978	Mr. P. Crilly	*OWENACURRA WIZARD*
		Br. Mr. M. Barry
		Hawkesburn John/Farmway Barley Gull
1979	Mr. D. P. Murphy	*HAWKESBURN JOHN*
		Br. Mrs. F. L. Marchant
		Hawkesburn Little John/Harvest Mouse
1987	Mr. D. P. Murphy	*ROSSTURC IVY*
		Br. Mrs. S. Milne
		Dandyhow Horlicks/Dandyhow Emily
	Dr. A.E.T. Sneeden	*ASTRA OF OPINAN*
		Uncle Walter of Dandyhow/ Tipalt Early Riser
1988	Mr. & Mrs. T. Nist	*ROSSTURC OONAGH*
		Br. Mrs. S. Milne
		Dandyhow Live Wire/Dandyhow Emily
1991	Mr. D. P. Murphy	*PLUSHCOURT TACTIC AT RATHVARRAIG*
		Br. Mrs. B. Judge
		Mansergh Doublet at Plushcourt/ Plushcourt on Target

SWEDEN, BY ANNA-KARIN BERGH, 1992

In Sweden, Border Terriers really prove to be all-round dogs. They are known to be suitable for almost everything that their owners would like to train them to do.

A lot of people in Sweden use them for hunting: birds, hares, badger, deer, and even elk. Foxes are rare in Sweden because of a nasty disease that killed almost every fox in this country, but they are coming back slowly. Several breeders are careful to breed only from stock that has the courage to fight a badger or a fox in the ground. There are special areas for training and competing. The most successful ones are often Show Champions as well. Borders are also used for blood tracking, which is searching in the woods for animals that have been

Swedish Ch. Redrob Jack the Knight.

damaged by cars or hurt when shot in a hunt. A Border Terrier
was the winner (all breeds) in the biggest competition of blood
tracking in 1990. The dog was, by the way, 13 years old.
Hunters all over Sweden give our dogs great credit for being
very good workers.

But Sweden is not only woods and wild animals, and in the
cities Border Terrier fans have found other work for their dogs
to do. At the moment, agility has become very popular,
especially among younger people. As one would expect,
Borders are perfect agility dogs. They are fast runners, they can
easily jump very high, they learn fast and they are happy to
play with their owners. The big Christmas Show in Stockholm
in December featured an agility race in which four Borders
were among the five best, and the winner was a Border Terrier
of course.

Other Borders have been successful in obedience classes. Every year we have at least one new obedience champion. Several are trained to be rescue dogs, and they search for people who have been buried under houses. Many people just keep their Border Terriers as their best companions, the best ones there are.

Our breed is slowly getting more and more popular. About 400 new Border Terriers are born every year, all of them KC registered. That makes them the third most popular in the Terrier Group, only Cairns and West Highland White Terriers are more numerous. At dog shows, Borders are often among the 10 largest entries of breeds at the show. On the whole, Border owners seem to be very active.

It all started in 1935, when a dog and a bitch came to Sweden from England. It was, however, not easy to sell puppies ("too ugly"), and today nothing is left of this blood-line. It was not until the '60s that the very few breeders had any success with this plain dog. In 1961, the *Bombax* kennel (Carl Gunnar Stafberg) and the *Juniper* kennel (Julie Geijer) bought one bitch puppy each out of the same litter, **Ch. Monkans Mikron** and **Ch. Monkans Mymlan**, and Swedish Borders of today carry lines back to these bitches. Kennel Bombax also imported **Ch. Leatty Panaga Tess**, who produced **Ch. Bombax Despot**, a well-known dog. Another famous dog was **Ch. Bombax Ericus Rex**, who was Best in Show at the SKC Jubilee Show in 1964 — first time in the world for a Border!

Today we have about 70 breeders, many of whom don't breed regularly. Over the years, new dogs have come to Sweden, almost all of them from England: **Ch. Rhosmerholme Amethyst, Dandyhow Sweet Polly, Ch. Daletyne Danny Boy, Ch. Clipstone Guardsman, Ch. Farmway Southern Hawk** (Finland), **Dandyhow Observer, Ch. Dandyhow Grenadier, Ch. Cheltorian Midnight** (by **Ch. Brannigan of Brumberhill**), **Ch. Clipstone Ceriph** and **Ch. Dykeside Jock Scott**. One Swedish dog, **Ch. Bombax Xavier**, was exported to England. From England to Norway came **Ch. Dandyhow Scotsman**.

All of these imports have meant a lot in improving the breed. At the moment the quality is quite good in Sweden. Top winning breeders are *Rabalder* (Anna-Karin Bergh) and *Tallarnas* (Mona Hedman), both of them breeding on Dandyhow lines. *Ottercap, Redrob* and *Gibas* have working Borders (badger) and

Swedish Border practicing Agility.

are also successful in the show rings. *Brackenhills* is another successful kennel. Both Bombax and Juniper are still breeding good dogs from their own lines. There are also several newcomers to the breed, whom we welcome.

We have a Swedish Border Terrier Club with more than 1,000 members. The club has a newsletter, which is very popular and is sent out four times a year. Once a year, the club arranges a big Border Terrier Club Show, which usually gets more entries

Top-winning Swedish Border of 1991 Rabalder Raka Spåret (grandson of Dandyhow Scotsman and great-grandson of Dandyhow Grenadier).

than any other show. Breed specialists are invited to judge, and it is a great honor to win at this event, where all the breeders and all the best dogs come, although it is not a championship show. At this show, Border fans from all over Sweden get a chance to meet each other. Your Border Terrier gives you friends, doesn't it?

NEW ZEALAND, BY ROSEMARY AND GEORGE WILLIAMSON

The difficulties and disappointments of trying to establish a new breed are well illustrated in the history of Border Terriers in New Zealand. Three times Borders were imported into New Zealand and within a few years there was no sign of their progeny.

The first recorded Kennel-Club-registered Border was an imported bitch, *Grener Bunty*, who was imported from England in 1947 by a Mrs. Green. Whether she had puppies or was just brought out as a pet will never be known. There were certainly no puppies registered with the Kennel Club.

In 1949, Pat Gilchrist imported a bitch in whelp, *Tweedside Red Soda*, and a dog *Tweedside Red Silvo,* and then in 1950, she imported another dog, **Beaucorn Bingo**. In 1951, she again imported a bitch in whelp, *Tweedside Red Echo*.

From this foundation stock, between 1950 and 1953 there were 31 registered puppies. Apart from one puppy that had a litter there is no record of any of the other puppies having any litters.

In 1954, Mr. E. A. Graham imported a bitch from Scotland, *Peggy of Glendearg*, and in 1956, he used a stud dog, **NZ Ch. Jim Bahadur**, owned by a Mrs. A. B. Cooke. As far as is known, she only had one litter. Mr. Cooke kept one of the bitch puppies from Peggy and mated her back to her sire, Jim Bahadur. This he did four times between 1960 and 1962.

In 1965, a Mr. Vicars imported a bitch in whelp, **Knavesmire Korowha**, but there were no subsequent litters.

However, better fortune was just around the corner. In 1965, Marion Forrester, who was a very well-known All Breeds judge and a breeder of Staffordshire Bull Terriers under her kennel name *Loggerheads*, decided to import a Border Terrier, **Hanleycastle Ruthless**, also a bitch, **Tippy of Petrina**. Tippy was made up to a NZ CH and then was mated by Hanleycastle Ruthless. The result was a litter of two dogs and a bitch. One of the dogs, **Loggerheads Tweed**, was twice put to an Australian Border, **Smethstowe BiggerIe**, and eight puppies were produced from these two litters. Several of these puppies were bred from by their new owners. Unfortunately, Marion Forrester was unable to continue with Tippy and she reluctantly decided to leave Borders and concentrate on her Staffordshire Bull Terriers.

In 1965, George and Rosemary Williamson migrated to New Zealand from England, and settled in Auckland, bringing **Cleo of the Hunt** and her son, **Red William**. Cleo's dam, **Leatty Lovely Queen**, had been mated to **UK Ch. Leatty Plough Boy** and on the advice of George Leatt, Cleo was then mated back to her sire. The resulting puppies were superb and **Red William** was a truly outstanding dog. Names of Borders - Xmas Box, Callum, Misty Dawn, Fearsome Belle, Alton Lad all figure in his pedigree.

It was not until 1973 that the Williamsons were in a position to show and breed. Their first import from England was from

Madeline Aspinwall — a bitch, *Farmway Swinging Chick*, by *Farmway Black Hawk* out of *Hobbykirk Barsac*.

Farmway Swinging Chick, known as *Chicko*, was mated to Red William and five puppies resulted. One bitch, **Patterdale Rhea**, was kept by the breeder and another bitch was sent to Mr. G. Massey in Australia. At this time, Australia was becoming very interested in the breed and in all, six Patterdale puppies of various pedigrees were sent to breeders there.

Between 1973 and 1982, Patterdale imported 10 Borders from England; these were *Farmway Swinging Chick, Farmway Tui, Farmway White Dove, Farmway Red Raven, Ribbleside Regent, Ribbleside Lady Love, Chevinor Ronoch, Foxhill Fenomenal, Headwaiter at Dormic* and *Dormic Mood Indigo*. This gave a large pool of genes and whilst line breeding was practiced there was no need to inbreed. All these dogs and bitches were made up to be champions.

It can be said that *Farmway Red Raven* put Border Terriers on the map of New Zealand when he won a Best in Show at an all breeds Championship Show at Kumeu in 1981. He had an excellent show record, winning 21 group awards at Championship Shows. He was also an excellent stud dog and his progeny have won and are winning many group awards.

Another outstanding dog was *Headwaiter at Dormic*, obtained from Mick and Doreen Rushby of Yorkshire. Mick was a gamekeeper and all his dogs were used for working. Headwaiter, or *Harry* as he was known, was a complete self showman and thoroughly enjoyed being shown on a loose lead. His only vice was in the Best of Group lineup: if a Pekinese or Bichon Frisé was in front of him he would think it was a fox for hunting.

Rosemary Williamson showed extensively between 1975 and 1989, and in that time her dogs won many group awards and several in show and reserve in show awards. Owing to ill health, her showing is now curtailed, but she is still breeding with four bitches.

In 1974, Marion Forrester had given Rosemary Williamson's name to James Graham as he had had a Border Terrier in Scotland. With some persuasion, he imported a dog, **Wilderscot Bandsman**, from Daphne Runsam. He was by **UK Ch. Clipstone Guardsman** out of **Farmway Blue Dove**. He also imported a bitch, *Farmway Swansdown*, bred by Madeline

Aspinwall, from *Farmway Red Puffin* by *Deerstone Despot Duty*. Unfortunately, after one litter Farmway Swansdown had to be spayed. The Grahams then imported from Mr. Beardwood, *Chevinor Raransay*, by *Ch. Ribbleside Ridgemen* out of *Chevinor Rosa*.

She was then put to *NZ Ch. Calypso of Patterdale* by *NZ Ch. Red William* out of *NZ Ch. Foxhill Fenomenal*. From a litter of four, a dog puppy, *Otterhead of Catcleuch*, was sent to Mary Whittington of Whakatane as a stud dog.

A mating between *NZ Ch. Wilderscot Bandsman* and *NZ Ch. Chevinor Raransay* took place in 1981, and a bitch puppy, *Otterhead of Ethelfrith*, was sent to Mrs. Pamela Hall-Jones as a breeding bitch. Jim Graham kept two bitches: *Otterhead of Ancroft* and *Otterhead of Blinkbonny*. Both these bitches had several litters. A dog puppy, *Otterhead of Dukesfield*, from *NZ CH Otterhead of Catcleuch* and *Otterhead of Ancroft*, was sent to Australia where he obtained his title and he has sired several litters.

From 1975 to 1990, Jim Graham and his *Otterhead* Kennels were very active both showing and breeding. Unfortunately, whilst still owning Borders he is no longer breeding them.

It can be said that the cooperation between Rosemary Williamson and her Patterdale Borders and Jim Graham and his Otterhead Borders firmly established Border Terriers in New Zealand. Both travelled the length and breadth of New Zealand showing together and getting Borders in front of judges and the public.

Borders in New Zealand were very popular as pets and some wonderful homes were found for puppies. It was not until 1978 that Mary Whittington, who was showing West Highland White Terriers under the kennel name of *Ladebraes*, obtained a Border Terrier dog, *Otterhead of Catcleuch*, from Jim Graham. He was by *NZ Ch. Calypso of Patterdale* out of *NZ Ch. Chevinor Raransay* (Imp UK). Later, she purchased from Jim Graham a bitch, *Otterhead of Kailzie*. Another bitch, *Ladebraes Laverock*, was from *Otterhead of Catcleuch* out of *Otterhead of Ancroft*. All these Borders have done well in group winnings and have helped to put Borders on the map. Mary lives in Whakatane, which is on the east coast of the Northern Island, midway between Auckland and Wellington.

In 1981, Mrs. Pamela Hall-Jones from Invercargill, in the south of the South Island, purchased a bitch puppy from J. Graham, *Otterhead of Ethelfrith*, and then mated her to *Patterdale's Red Raven* and subsequently to Raven's son, *Patterdale Ring Dove*. All her puppies are placed locally. Her kennel name is *Ben Bhraggie*, after her Scottish homeland.

In 1983, Brenda Carrodus in Christchurch, in the middle of the South Island, purchased a dog puppy for showing from Rosemary Williamson, *Rushby of Patterdale*. He was by *NZ Ch. Headwaiter at Dormic* out of *NZ Ch. Dormic Mood Indigo*. She then bought a bitch puppy from Otterhead Kennels, *Otterhead of Sweethorpe*, by *Ch. Otterhead of Catcleuch* out of *Ch. Otterhead of Blinkbonny* and has had several litters and has shown. Her kennel name is *Bordersweet*.

Slowly, the number of breeders was increasing. In 1985, Anna McHaughton obtained a bitch puppy from Noeline Taylor, who had imported a bitch, *Rhozzum Virtue*, from P. D. Sharp in England. She then mated her to *NZ Ch. Otterhead of Catcleuch* and she is still having occasional litters.

Also in 1985, Julie Clarke of *Lester Kennels* in Marton near Wellington, a breeder of Australian Terriers and Bull Terriers, was judging in Australia when she came in contact with a Border Terrier belonging to Mrs. Margaret Burgoine, *Aust. Ch. Bracklyn Bijouse*, a descendant of one of Patterdale Borders sent to Australia. She fell in love with her and took her back to New Zealand to show and make her up. Whilst here, she was mated to Mary Whittington's dog, *NZ Ch. Otterhead of Catcleuch*, and then returned to Australia. Julie then had one of the bitch puppies, *Bodalla Fen Windmill*, whom she made up to NZ CH. She has won several group awards. She is breeding and showing extensively and should further the breed in the future. She has recently obtained *Patterdale Mini Max*. He was by *Patterdale Dowgill* out of *NZ Ch. Inca Dove of Patterdale*. Julie is now five generations away from *Bracklyn Bijouse*.

In 1985, Gail O'Keefe of *Tennille Kennels* was given a Border Terrier puppy for her birthday. Her parents bred and showed Bull Terriers, and this puppy, *Teca of Patterdale*, from *NZ Ch. Inca Dove of Patterdale* was made up to champion status in 12 months and was Dog of the Year in 1986 with the Canterbury Terrier Club, and won many group awards. Teca's first litter was by *NZ Ch. Headwaiter at Dormic* (Imp UK), and there were six puppies. Gail kept a bitch puppy, **Tennille Queen Victoria**, another bitch puppy went to Brenda Carrodus of Bordersweet and a dog puppy, **Tennille our Silvester**, went to Julie Clarke of Lester Kennels.

Teca's next litter was by **NZ Ch. Rushby of Petterdale** and a dog puppy went to her sister Diane O'Keefe. Teca's last litter was by **NZ & Aust. Ch. Brigand of Brockhole** and **Lynsett** (Imp UK). There were two bitch puppies: one went to Brenda Carrodus and the other, **Tennile My Sweet Dore**, was kept by Gail. She has been made up to champion and has won group awards.

Gail also owns in partnership with her sister, Diane, a bitch, **Patterdale Briganza**, out of **Patterdale Daidor** by **NZ & Aust. Ch. Brigand of Brockhole and Lynsett** (Imp UK).

In 1990, Andrea Herd of Wanganui obtained a bitch puppy from Julie Clarke. Then her parents, breeders of Beagles under the name of *Tamaleigh*, went to England and obtained a dog puppy, **Firgate Robert at Tamaleigh**, by **Plushcourt Run the Gauntlett** out of **Fingate Rowena of Sprignell**. He is a very promising dog and should help the breed. He has been mated to Andrea's bitch and puppies are expected shortly.

There are several other owners whose bitches have either had a litter or are contemplating one. So hopefully, the Border is here to stay in New Zealand, but it will need determination and dedication of the few current breeders for the breed to survive. One of the problems is the distance between breeders and the high cost of flying dogs around New Zealand. As yet, we have no Border Terrier Club, but it could well be that the time is approaching when this could be a possibility.

PART IV

Reference Material

- *Appendices*

- *Glossary*

- *Bibliography*

- *Index*

APPENDIX A

GOLD REGISTER OF MERIT DOGS

DOGS	OWNER	BREEDER
Ch. Portholme Max Factor	Dalquest	Mrs S Mulcaster
Ch. Portholme Mhor of Dalquest	Dalquest	Mrs S Mulcaster
Ch. Portholme Macsleap of Dalquest	Dalquest	Mrs S Mulcaster
Ch. Little Fir Kirksman	M Alvord, B Finley	D Kline
Ch. Rob Roy's Buckler	M Scott	L &E Hammett
Ch. Workmore Waggoner	K Seeman	Mrs C Walker
Ch. Duttonlea Autocrat of Dandyhow	N Hughes	W Wrigley
Ch. Little Fir Gremlin of Ariel	K & P Klothen	D Kline
Ch. Ketka Swashbuckler	C Sowders, H Gosselin	Sowders & Tinker
Ch. Oldstone Ragrug	R & R A Naun	R & R A Naun
Ch. Sprignell Woodsmoke	J & C Wheeler	Mrs S W Clarkson
Ch. Solo	M Scott	M Scott
Ch. Seabrook Spriggan	B & L Anthony	B & L Anthony
Ch. Foxley Bright Forecast	B Finley	P Quinn & C Moon
Ch. Scooter	M Scott	M Scott
Ch. Thoraldby Magic Chip	P Quinn	P Thompson
Ch. Traveler of Foxley	B Kemp	P Quinn
Ch. Woodlawn's Dusky Gentleman	D Corl	B Finley
Ch. Todfield Trafalgar Square	D Kline	D Kline
Ch. Trails End Buddy of Glenfarm	Wallace & Hughes	N Hughes
Ch. Ryswick Remember Me	B Blake	A Willis

BITCHES	OWNER	BREEDER
Ch. Dalquest Dare's Dancer	J & E Barker	M Harvey
Ch. Shuttle	M Scott	S Mitchell
Ch. Trails End Peaceful Bree UD	J Frier	N Hughes
Ch. Dalquest Rebeca of Woodlawn	B Finley	Dalquest
Ch. Edenbrae Dusky Maiden	B Finley & M Pickford	Mrs M Edgar
Ch. Ketka Gopher Broke	C Sowders & D Tinker	C Sowders & K Zimmel
Ch. Ketka Short Circuit	C Sowders	C Sowders
Ch. Trails End Bewitched	K Blake	N Hughes
Ch. Red Eft's Eowyn of Rohan	B LaPointe	N Hiscock & J Frier-Murza
Ch. Woodlawn's Prime Time	B Finley	B Finley
Ch. Standish's Dynamite	J Strassels & J Standish	J, M, & D M Standish

APPENDIX B

ABBREVIATIONS

Titles awarded by the American Kennel Club:
CD - Companion Dog
CDX - Companion Dog Excellent

CH - Conformation Champion
UD - Utility Dog
OTCH - Obedience Champion
TD - Tracking Dog
TDX - Tracking Dog Excellent

Awards given by the American Working Terrier Association:
WC - Working Certificate
HC - Hunting Certificate
CG - Certificate of Gameness
Additional initials of TT indicate that the dog has been temperament tested.

APPENDIX C

REGISTRATIONS BY YEAR

Year		Year		Year	
1930	6	1957	53	1984	276
1931	None	1958	47	1985	383
1932	12	1959	64	1986	346
1933	4	1960	43	1987	468
1934	4	1961	70	1988	500
1935	49	1962	47	1989	521
1936	2	1963	49	1990	510
1937	None	1964	61	1991	657
1938	13	1965	51		
1939	11	1966	76		
1940	19	1967	57		
1941	3	1968	51		
1942	9	1969	61		
1943	10	1970	39		
1944	6	1971	59		
1945	6	1972	58		
1946	6	1973	74		
1947	28	1974	71		
1948	14	1975	93		
1949	21	1976	104		
1950	16	1977	110		
1951	12	1978	136		
1952	34	1979	163		
1953	27	1980	207		
1954	30	1981	249		
1955	21	1982	272		
1956	39	1983	265		

APPENDIX D

Some other active breeders not detailed in text:

Applegarth - Mary C. Opperman, New Hill NC

Arundel - Al & Lois Langish, Bordentown NJ

Beaverwood - Nancy Kloskowski, Chicago IL

Briarwood - Pattie & Suzanne Pfeffer, Bakersfield CA
Chadwick - Don and Barb Catlin, Chagrin Falls OH
Circle B - Susan and Joe Berman, Free Union VA
Cymri Hill - Catherine Murphy, Bradford MA
Dalfox - James & Helen Ham, Sterling Heights MI
Deswind - Robin Young, Mesa AZ
Dickendall - Kendall Herr, Catasauqua PA
Do-A-Little - Deborah Rafacz, Crown Point IN
Foxfire - Teddi Beardsley, Bellaire TX
Foxmoore - Judith Gilman, Warrenton VA
Hickory Ridge - Bob and Arden LeBlanc, Galena OH
High Dyke - Camilla Moon, Ipswich MA
JA-CA-B - Janice Cook, Shreveport LA
Jollymuff - Diane Jones, Mt. Holly NJ
Lerner, Renée, Englewood Cliff NJ
Levy, Mr. and Mrs Edwin Jr., Richmond VA
Madcap - Marian and David Stone, Urbana IL
Norbury - Jennifer Chambers, Stowe VT
Reveille - Damara Bolté, Leesburg VA
Rongevar - Janet Ek, White Bear Lake MN
St. Andrews - Elizabeth King and Charles Oldham, Lake Oswego OR
Stonehaven - James Lenahan, Dayton OH
Sunkist - Harriet Wallace, Chino Valley AZ
Terraholm - Laurel Tofflemire, Coos Bay OR
Terrasong - Darlene G. Morton, Phoenix AZ
The - Jim Kane, Sebastopol CA
Tweed Hill - Donald and Brenda Werbelow, La Habra Heights CA
Vabrook - Jimmie & Frank Brooking, Shreveport LA

The authors apologize for any errors or omissions of breeders who have become active since this list was compiled, or of breeders from whom we received no information.

APPENDIX E

Border Terrier Organizations:

Border Terrier Club of America
Ms. Jean Clark
441 Sugar Hill Rd. South
Weare NH 03281

Border Terrier Club of the Redwoods
Linda Boch
24495 Sherwood Road
Willits CA 95490-9502

Border Terrier Fanciers of the West
Brenda Werbelow
1965 Chota Road
La Habra Heights CA 90631

Cascade Border Terrier Club
Mrs. Anita Moran
PO Box 7314
Ketchikan AK 99901

Great Lakes Border Terrier Club
Mrs. Laurale Stern
832 Lincoln Blvd.
Manitowoc WI 54220

Lone Star Border Terrier Fanciers
James Rydberg
832 Lake Forest Court
Grapevine TX 76051

Northeast Border Terrier Club
Mrs. Carlie Krolick
132 Ridgecrest Rd.
Briarcliff Manor NY 10510

THE AMERICAN WORKING TERRIER ASSOCIATION

The American Working Terrier Association (AWTA) was formed in May 1971, by Patricia Adams Lent. An objective of the AWTA is to encourage and preserve the natural instinct of the earth Terriers, which is to enter an underground earth and react in a positive manner when facing the quarry. Numerous trials are held across the country throughout the year. The AWTA issues *Certificates of Gameness* to dogs qualifying at trials in the Open Division, *Hunting Certificates* to dogs used regularly for hunting over the period of one year, and *Working Certificates* to dogs qualifying for work in a natural den. Another objective of the AWTA is to encourage and preserve the natural hunting abilities of all Terriers in above-ground sport.

BREEDS RECOGNIZED BY THE AWTA

For the purpose of AWTA trials, an earth breed is a dog of the correct size and character to enter a nine-inch artificial earth. The AWTA recognizes these breeds: Australian, Bedlington, Border, Cairn, Dandie Dinmont, Fox, Lakeland, Norwich, Norfolk, Scottish, Sealyham, Skye, Welsh, West Highland White, Dachshunds, Jack Russell Terrier, Jadg Terriers and Patterdales.

For the purpose of hunting, both in natural earth and above ground, the AWTA recognizes the above breeds and all of the larger AKC Terrier breeds.

WORKING CERTIFICATE:

This certificate is awarded only to dogs whose owners are AWTA members in good standing at the time of qualifying work. Only one Working Certificate (WC) is awarded per dog.

The WC is issued to a Terrier or Dachshund who has worked in a natural earth to one of the following quarry: woodchuck, fox, raccoon, or badger. This does not include work in a drain or otherwise man-made earth. The dog must enter the earth without encouragement and disappear into the earth. He must work down to the quarry and cause it to bolt, or draw it from the earth. If the quarry does not bolt or it is not drawn, the Terrier must hold it at bay. There is to be no doubt that the dog is right up to the quarry. If the dog is not dug to, he must show evidence of a face-to-face encounter with bites or quarry fur in his mouth. The baying must be continuous for at least three minutes.

The Terrier or Dachshund must work by the above rules and his work must be witnessed by another AWTA member.

HUNTING CERTIFICATE:

This certificate is awarded only to dogs whose owners are AWTA members in good standing during the entire period of qualifying work. Only one Hunting Certificate is awarded per dog.

This certificate is issued to dogs regularly used for hunting such game as woodchucks, rabbits, squirrels, opossums, rats, raccoons, muskrats, or for flushing and/or retrieving upland birds. Game must either be killed by the dog or shot by his hunting partner. A dog must spend a full season hunting before this certificate is issued. A season is whatever time is allowed by state hunting regulations when the species is controlled by state game laws.

CERTIFICATE OF GAMENESS:

This certificate is awarded to the dog who qualifies with a score of 100 percent in an Open Class at an AWTA sanctioned trial. The dog is required to travel a 30-foot earth, reaching the quarry within 30 seconds (50 percent). The dog must then work the quarry, as defined on the judge's score sheet, continuously for a full 60 seconds (50 percent).

The handler may give one command on release, then must stand quietly at the release point throughout the test. Time in the Open Class is started when the dog is released. The dog may enter the earth, come out, and re-enter, providing he does not go all the way to the quarry. He is not penalized as long as he reaches the quarry within 30 seconds from the time of release. Once the dog reaches the quarry, he must not leave it; if he does, he receives no score for working even though he may return to the quarry.

If the dog reaches the quarry within 30 seconds and works the quarry continuously for a full minute, he earns his Certificate of Gameness.

Afterbirth — The placenta attached to the sac in which puppy is born.

American Kennel Club (AKC) — The governing and registration body along with the United Kennel Club for purebred dogs.

AKC Gazette — A monthly publication of the AKC containing articles, statistics about shows and registrations and official and proposed actions of the AKC.

All-Breed Club — A club devoted to the showing and breeding of purebred dogs. Membership is open to breeders and exhibitors of all breeds. Holds championship shows.

All-Breed Show — An AKC-approved show in which all AKC-approved breeds can be exhibited.

Artificial Insemination — Impregnating a bitch with frozen or extended sperm.

Back — That portion of the topline starting just behind the withers and ending where the croup and loin join.

Backcrossing — To cross a first generation hybrid with one of the parents.

Baiting — Keeping a dog alert in the ring through the use of food or a favorite toy.

Balance — Overall fitting of the various parts of the dog to give a picture of symmetry and correct interaction.

Best Of Breed — Best of that breed in an all-breed or specialty show In the all-breed show it goes on to compete for higher awards.

Best In Show — Top award in an all-breed show.

Best Of Variety — Top award for breeds that are divided by variety based on coat, color or size.

Best Of Winners — Defeats other sex winner. Captures that sex's points if greater than its own on that day.

Bitch — A female dog.

Bite	Position of upper and lower teeth in relation to each other. Various breed standards call for different kinds of bite often based on function.
Bloodline	A specific strain or type within a breed.
Bottle Feeding	Using a doll bottle to feed formula to a newborn puppy.
Breech Presentation	Puppy born feet first rather than head first. Can cause whelping difficulties as puppy may get turned sideways in the birth canal.
Breed Ring	Exhibition area where dogs are judged by breed.
Brucellosis	A sexually transmitted disease or infection.
Bulbus Glandis	A portion of the penis closest to the testicles which fills with blood to three times its size during the sexual act. It serves to "tie" the male and female together while the male ejaculates sperm.
Cesarean Section	Removing puppies from the womb surgically.
Campaigning A Dog	Seriously exhibiting a champion to compete for top honors in his breed, group and top 10 all-breed honors.
Canine Herpes Virus	An infection in puppies caused by an infected dam. A leading cause of puppy mortality.
Canine Parvovirus	Myocardial forms attack only puppies. Severe, often fatal reaction. Cardial form attacks older dogs.
Championship	A title earned by winning 15 points under AKC rules, including two major awards of 3, 4 or 5 points under two different judges.
Championship Points	Awarded on the basis of the number of dogs competing by sex and breed. Each part of the country has a different point rating based upon previous year's entries. Maximum number of points per show is 5. Fifteen are needed for a championship, with two major awards among them.

Chromosome	Cell nucleus of all multicell organisms that contain DNA. Comprising the genes of that species.
Colostrum	A part of the bitch's milk which provides puppies immunity from many viral and bacterial diseases.
Contour	Silhouette or profile, form or shape.
Conformation	The form and structure of the various parts to fit a standard.
Crate	A metal, plastic or wood kennel (in various sizes). Dogs may sleep and travel in them.
Cropped	Trimming the ears to fit a breed pattern.
Cryptorchid	A male dog with neither testicle descended. Ineligible to compete at AKC shows.
Dam	Mother of a litter of puppies.
Degeneration	Used in reference to inbreeding. After primary generations, stock shows reduction in size, bone and vigor.
Dehydration	Loss of body fluids - may lead to death.
Developmental Phases	Stages through which puppies grow.
Dew Claws	Hardy nails above pastern. Most breeds have them removed. In many breeds they are not present.
DNA	Deoxyribonucleic acid - genes are made up of DNA. They are regarded as the building blocks of life.
Dominant	Color or characteristic that covers up all others which are recessive to it.
Docking	The clipping off of the tail to a prescribed length to meet a breed standard.
Dropper-feeding	Feeding formula to newborn puppies through the use of a small medicine dropper.
Eclampsia	An attack of convulsions during and after pregnancy.
Egg	A female reproductive cell.

Estrus	Period of bitch's heat cycle when she is ready to breed.
Exhibitors	People who show their dogs.
Expression	Facial aspect or countenance.
Eye For A Dog	An old dog game expression meaning the ability to select a good dog without a lot of effort.
Fading Puppy Syndrome	A malnourished puppy due to loss of electrolytes. May lead to death.
Fallopian Tubes	Conduits for eggs from ovary to uterus.
Fetus	The growing puppy within the womb.
Filial Regression	The tendency of offspring to regress toward mediocrity if controlled breeding is not carried out.
Finishable	A dog capable of completing its championship.
Forechest	The point of the thorax that protrudes beyond the point of the shoulder.
Foreface	That part of the muzzle from just below the forehead to the nose.
Gaiting	Walking or trotting a dog to discern proper movement.
Gene	The smallest unit of hereditary information.
Genetics	The study of the science of heredity.
Genotype	Genetic term meaning the unseen genetic makeup of the dog.
Gestation	The organic development of the puppy within the uterus.
Gravity	The pull of the earth upon a body.
Groom	To comb, clip and brush a dog.
Grooming Table	A specially designed (often foldable) table with matting for grooming and training dogs.
Handler	Person showing the dog.

Heat	A bitch coming into season so she can be bred. Usually twice a year.
Heredity	The sum of what a dog inherits from preceding generations.
Hetrozygous	Non-dominant for a trait or color. Carries both dominant and recessive genes for a variety of traits.
Homozygous	Dominant for a trait or color. Carries no recessive for that characteristic.
Hybrid	Dogs who have gene pairs — non-dominant.
Hybrid Vigor	The extra vigor or development exhibited by offspring of an outcross.
Hyperthermia	A chilling of the puppies which is liable to cause death.
Inbreeding	Very close familial breeding, i.e., brother X sister, father X daughter or son X mother.
Inguinal Ring	Muscles of the abdominal cavity (groin) that prevent adult testes from going back up into abdominal cavity and, which can prevent their proper descent in puppies.
Judge	A person approved by AKC or UKC to judge various breeds.
Labor	The act of attempting to whelp puppies.
Lead	A strap or cord fastened around dog's neck to guide him. Also called leash.
Lead Training	Teaching the dog to walk and trot properly so as to best exhibit his conformation. May also be used for control.
Line Breeding	Breeding closely within a family of dogs, i.e., grandfather to granddaughter.
Match Show	A practice show that serves as a training ground for young dogs, prospective judges and members of the dog club holding the show.
Malnutrition	Lacking the proper nourishment to provide normal healthy growth.

Gregor Mendel	A monk in 19th Century Czechoslovakia who discovered the mathematical formulas for the inheritance of color and size in sweet peas and launched the science of genetics.
Metritis	A uterine infection in the dam that can transmit bacterial infection to an entire litter.
Monorchid	A male dog with only one testicle descended. Ineligible to compete in AKC shows.
Monstrosities	Severe, often lethal deviations from expected structure, usually brought out through inbreeding.
Nasal Aspirator	A suction device for sucking mucous from infant puppies' nasal passages.
Natural Selection	Charles Darwin's theory of how species evolve.
Neonatal	New born.
Neonatal Septecemia	An infection in newborn puppies picked up by staphylococcus germs in the dam's vaginal tract.
Non-Dominant	An animal with characteristics that are mostly recessive.
Nucleus	The center of a cell. Contains chromosomes and is essential to all cell functions, such as cell division for reproduction.
Outcrossing	Matings of animals that are somewhat inbred to unrelated animals to reinstate vigor and substance.
Ovulation	The female process of creating eggs for reproduction.
Ovum	An egg ready for sperm to fertilize it.
Parasites	Infestations of lice, ticks or fleas as well as internal infestation of various worms.
Pastern	The body's shock absorber. Located at the juncture where the paw meets foreleg.
Pedigree	Hierarchical listing of ancestors. Best used when combined with photos and anecdotal data.

Phenotype	The actual outward appearance as can be seen— opposite of genotype.
Placenta	A vascular organ that links the fetus to the dam's uterus. Nourishes and mediates fetal change. Also known as an afterbirth.
Plaining Out	Usually occurs as head changes because of the loss of puppy teeth.
Postpartum	After birth.
Pounding	Results when front stride is shorter than rear. Hindquarter thrust forces front feet to strike the ground before they are fully prepared to absorb shock.
Pregnant	Term used for bitch carrying puppies.
Producing Power	The ability to stamp one's get with positive features of championship caliber.
Proestrus	First part of heat cycle.
Profile	Outline or silhouette.
Proportion	Relationship, ratio of one body part to another.
Proven Sire	Male dog that has enough offspring to judge his potency.
Puppy Septicemia	Bacterial infection caused by a mastitis infection in the dam. Often fatal if not treated immediately.
Purebred	A dog whose sire and dam are of the same breed and whose lineage is unmixed with any other breed.
Quarantine	A period in which a dog is isolated from other animals while being observed for communicable diseases.
Recessive	Color or trait which is not dominant and must link up with another recessive for expression.
Reserve Winners	Dog or bitch that is runner up to the winner. May gain points if winner is ineligible or is disqualified.
Ribs	The thoracic vertebrae that surround the heart and lungs.

Sac	Membrane housing puppy within uterus.
Scrotum	Housing for male dogs testicles.
Show Pose	Setting a dog in a position to exhibit its conformation. Also called stacking.
Showmanship	The bravura exhibition of a dog.
Sire	Father of a litter.
Special	A champion dog or bitch competing for
Best of Breed or Best of Variety award	A class for champions only.
Specialty Club	A club devoted to fanciers of one specific breed of dog.
Specialty Show	An AKC-approved show for members of a single breed only.
Spermatozoa	Motile sperm from male dog.
Spoon-Feeding	Slowly feeding milk formula to baby puppy using a small spoon.
Stacking	See Show Pose.
Standard	An official description of the breed developed by that breed's parent club and approved by AKC.
Structural Design	The blueprint from which the originators of a breed sought to create a dog for the task at hand.
Subcutaneous Muscle	That type of muscle which lies directly under the skin.
Symmetry	A pleasing balance of all parts.
Test Breeding	A mating usually of a parent of unknown genotype and one of a known genotype to reveal what characteristics the unknown one will throw.
Tie	The locking together of the dog and bitch during mating caused by the swelling of the Bulbis Glandis just behind the penis bone.
Topline	That portion of the dog's outline from the withers to the set on of the tail.

Toxic Milk Syndrome	Toxic bacteria in dam's milk having a toxic effect on nursing puppies.
Tube-Feeding	Inserting a tube down the esophagus into the puppy's stomach to release milk formula slowly.
Type	Characteristics distinguishing a breed.
Unbroken Line	A pedigree line of continuous producers down to the current sire or dam.
Umbilical cord	A cord that connects the fetus with the placenta attaching at the puppy's navel.
Vaccinations	Shots administered to ward off certain diseases.
Vulva	External parts (lips) of bitch's genital organs.
Wean	Gradually changing puppies to solid food away from mother's milk.
Whelping Box	Where you wish to have the litter born and the bitch doesn't. Used later for nursing bitch and her puppies.
Winners (Dog & Bitch)	Best from all the competing classes. Wins points toward championship.
Withers	Highest point on the shoulder blades.

BIBLIOGRAPHY AND SOURCES

American Kennel Club Gazette

American Kennel Club Studbooks

Bierman, Ann, "Feeding Your Puppy," *The Golden Retriever Review*, March 1987.

Book of Dogs. Official Publication of the Canadian Kennel Club, Toronto: General Publishing, 1982.

Border Reporter. Great Lakes Border Terrier newsletter.

Borderline, The. Border Terrier Club of America newsletter.

Breed Books 1 - 7. Border Terrier Club of America.

Burns, Marcia & Margaret N. Fraser, *Genetics of the Dog*, Philadelphia: J. B. L. Lippincott, 1966.

Clark, Ross D. & Joan R. Stainer, *Medical & Genetic Aspects of Purebred Dogs*, Edwardsville, KS: Vet. Med. Pub. Co., ,1983.

Clothier, Suzanne, "Selecting for Vigor," *AKC Gazette*, June 1987.

Complete Dog Book, The. Official Publication of the American Kennel Club, 18th Edition, New York:Howell Book House, 1992.

Done, S. H. et al, *Hemivertebrae in the Dog: Clinical and Pathological Observations*, Vet Rec 96: 1975, 313-317.

Down to Earth. American Working Terrier Association newsletter.

Fox, Michael W., *Understanding Your Dog*, New York: Coward, McCann & Geoghegan, 1972.

Freak, M. J., *Abnormal Conditions Associated with Pregnancy and Parturition in the Bitch*, 1962, Vet 74: 1323-1335.

Furumoto, Howard H., "Frozen and Extended Semen," *The Ilio*, Hawaii's Dog News, Oct. & Nov., 1986.

Gardner, Walter. *About the Border Terrier*, Bradford, MA: Bradford Press, 1985.

Grossman, Alvin, "The Basis of Heredity," *AKC Gazette*, April 1980.

Grossman, Alvin & Beverly Grossman, *Winning With Purebred Dogs —
Design for Success*, Doral Publishing, Wilsonville, OR, 1991.

Hancock, David. *Old Working Dogs*, Aylesbury, England: Shire
Publications, 1984.

Holst, Phyllis A., *Canine Reproduction — A Breeder's Guide*. Loveland,
CO:Alpine Publications, 1985.

Hutt, Frederick B. *Genetics for Dog Breeders*, San Francisco: W. H.
Freeman & Co., 1979.

Jackson, Frank and Irving, W. Ronald. *The Border Terrier*, London: W.
and G. Foyle, 1979.

Kirk, Robert W. *Current Veterinary Therapy IX - Small Animal Practice*,
Philadelphia:W. B. Saunders Co., 1986.

Kirk, Robert W., & S. I. Bistner. *Handbook of Veterinary Procedures and
Emergency Treatment, Hereditary Defects of Dogs*, Table 124.,
Philadelphia:W. B. Saunders, 1985.

Mohrman, R.K., "Supplementation — May be Hazardous to Your
Pet's Health," *The Great Dane Reporter*, April 1980.

Nebzydoski, J. A., "Ischemic necrosis of the femoral head in dogs: a
review." *Vet Med & SAC*, (1982) 77 (4) pp 631-632, 634-637.

Orme, Hester G., "Color from Puppy to Adult," Border Terrier Club
of America *1971 Breed Booklet*, 1972, pp 28-29.

Orme, Hester G. *Border Terrier Champions and Challenge Certificate
Winners*, 1953.

Patterson, Donald F., & R. L Pyle, "Genetic Aspects of Congenital
Heart Disease in Dogs," *Newer Knowledge about Dogs*, 1971, Proc 21st
Gaines Vet Symp, Ames. IA 20-28.

Pough, Margaret B., "Coat Color Genetics in the Border Terrier,"
Border Terrier Club of America 1971 Breed Booklet, 1972, pp 31-34.

Roslin-Williams, Anne. *The Border Terrier*, London: H. F. and G.
Hitherby, 1976.

Ross, George D., DVM, Ithaca, NY, pers. comm., 1986.

Rubin, L.F. *Inherited Eye Diseases in Purebred Dogs*, Baltimore:Williams
& Wilkins,1989.

" Telltale Gene, The," *Consumer Reports*, July 1990.

Willis, Malcolm B. *Genetics of the Dog*, London: H.F. Witherby, Ltd., 1989.

Wittels, Bruce R., "Nutrition of the Newly Born and Growing Individuals, " *The Great Dane Reporter*, Jan/Feb 1985.

SUGGESTED ADDITIONAL READING

Collins, Donald F., *The Collins Guide to Dog Nutrition*, New York: Howell Book House, 1987.

Gardner, Walter J.F., *About the Border Terrier*, Bradford, MA: Bradford Press, 1985.

Horner, Tom, *Terriers of the World*, London: Faber and Faber, 1984.

Jackson, Jean and Frank, *All About the Border Terrier*, London: Pelham Books, 1989.

Kay, William J., DVM, *Complete Book of Dog Health*, New York: Howell Book House, 1990.

Rutherford, Clarice and Neil, David, *How To Raise A Puppy You Can Live With*, Loveland, CO: Alpine Publications, 1981.

Shaw, Michael, *The Modern Working Terrier*, Suffolk, England: Boydell Press, 1985.

Spira, Harold R., *Canine Terminology*, New York: Howell Book House, 1985.

Walkowicz, Chris and Wilcox, Bonnie DVM, *Successful Dog Breeding*, New York: Arco Publishing, 1985.

INDEX